crazy for God

crazy for God

christopher edwards

Prentice-Hall, Inc., Englewood Cliffs, New Jersey

Book Design by Joan Ann Jacobus
Art Director: Hal Siegel

Crazy for God by Christopher Edwards

Printed in the United States of America
Prentice-Hall International, Inc., London/Prentice-Hall of Australia, Pty.
Ltd., Sydney/Prentice-Hall of Canada, Ltd., Toronto/Prentice-Hall of India
Private Ltd., New Delhi/Prentice-Hall of Japan, Inc., Tokyo/Prentice-Hall of
Southeast Asia Pte. Ltd., Singapore/Whitehall Books Limited, Wellington,
New Zealand
10   9   8   7   6   5   4   3   2

Library of Congress Cataloging in Publication Data

Edwards, Christopher
  Crazy for God.

  1. Edwards, Christopher, 1954-   2. Segye
Kiddokyo Tongil Sillyŏng Hyŏphoe—Biography.
I. Title.
BX9750.S4E37   248'.24   78-31632
ISBN 0-13-188979-6

this book is written in gratitude to Galen and Liz Kelly for the support they gave me upon my leaving the cult and their patience in guiding me through my most difficult months; to Dr. Hardat Sukhdeo, whose compassion and wisdom enabled me to recover my mind and will; to the former cult members of this country who dare speak out about a terror so real and so new to an astonished and unbelieving public; to Mariana Fitzpatrick and the staff of Prentice-Hall for their excellent editorial assistance and their willingness to publish such controversial material. But most of all I want to thank my father and mother for making an impossibly difficult choice and carrying it through so well, risking the anguish of persecution for the sake of my future well-being. Thank you for showing me the power and depth of human love. Thank you for saving my life.

99892

contents

foreword/

This book is about the rapid near-destruction of a human-being—myself. It is the story of the deceit, manipulation and terror which thousands of young Americans experience daily at the hands of modern cults. Although a different group was involved, I believe it is also a story which may help to explain the paranoia and absolute obedience which led to the recent horror of the People's Temple murders and mass suicide.

My story began innocently enough when I was lured into a "fun" weekend in June of 1975 on a farm owned by a front group for Sun Myung Moon's Unification Church in Berkeley, California. It ended seven and a half months later on a Saturday afternoon in mid-January with a dramatic kidnapping and deprogramming engineered by my father and a team of hired professionals.

In the following pages, I describe the sinister indoctrination process by which I was transformed from an intelligent, independent human being into a completely subservient disciple of my new Messiah—terrified of questioning, dependent on my leaders for my every move, ready and willing to die or even kill to restore the world under the absolute rule of Reverend Moon. I share with you the degradation I experienced as I rose in the ranks of the Moon organization to become an "adopted" son of the two most powerful cult leaders in America. I describe my losing battle to retain my mind and will in a world of structured madness.

This has been a difficult and painful book to write. I have had to relive every nightmare connected with those seven months with the Moonies in order to re-create for you the horrors I experienced. You may be amused at first by the absurdities that Moonies mouth and actually believe, but it will soon become chillingly clear that beneath the smiley faces and baby songs lies a systematic plan for rapid subjugation for the Cause.

Everything in this story is true although it is obviously impossible to reproduce the dialogue and thoughts of characters verbatim. Some personalities and events have been compressed or conjoined for the sake of readability, but everything that I describe happened to me and is typical of a Moonie's experience, however much the cult leaders may deny this. All the names in this book with the exception of Moon's have been changed to protect the guilty, among whom are some of the most innocent victims of all.

As a former Moonie, I am aware of Unification Church tactics toward those who dare expose its secrets. But no risk seems too great if CRAZY FOR GOD prevents a few more families from being destroyed and a few more minds from being bent and twisted in the name of love.

crazy for God

prologue/

I began to cry. My stomach churned and I wanted to vomit. Waves of bitterness engulfed me, turning my anguish into hatred for the strange faces around me.

I looked at the figure slumped in the corner, a weary old man who happened to be my father. Crumpled in a chair, head resting in his hands, he looked exhausted and miserable. I raised my finger and thrust it toward him shouting: "You just don't know what you're doing. I'm not your son anymore. I am a son of God! You'll pay for this. I swear you will."

"My God, is this my son?" he murmured. "What have they done to him?" He shook his head.

"Why? Why are you doing this?" I cried. "Why are you interfering with my life? Why are you trying to take away everything that's important to me? Why? Why?"

I wiped my sweaty palms on my legs and turned my chair to face him. Silence, followed by words that cut steel.

1

"Chris, you're very sick. You don't realize what they've done to you. You need help, and we're here to help you."

"We? These hired thugs? You ally yourself with professional kidnappers, haters of God? You're all my enemies."

"Chris, you've got to listen to me. I'm sorry, but I just had no choice. Please cooperate and it will be over soon. Please believe me. Trust us."

"That's it, Doc. We're with ya. Keep it comin'," said one of the thugs, the tall, scruffy young man who had held me down in the kidnapper's car. My father bowed his head.

The kidnapping had taken place two hours before. Now, after a long, frightening ride from Berkeley to Richmond, California, we were locked in a darkened Holiday Inn room, five men and myself. I had soon figured out that the room next door had also been rented by the thugs, for I could hear people leaving and returning.

I sank back into my chair, silently chanting: "Heavenly Father, save me from Satan!" The words tumbled through my brain, over and over, faster and faster, circling frantically before my mind's eye. As if in answer, I seemed to hear a voice say: "The Family will save you. Heavenly Father is with you." I chanted harder, digging my nails into the fabric of the chair. O Heavenly Father, save me! In True Parents' name I pray.

The silent chanting calmed me somewhat and I glanced again at my father. Dressed in his Eisenhower suit, he was gazing blankly at one of the thugs. Just who was this father of mine? I knew my memory was spotty. I knew it and it scared me. But doubtless that was the price of living for God. And I had given my mind to God, had offered it up on his sacred altar. But still I was troubled by the disconnected images that persisted in dancing and flickering across my mind, images of my mother taking me to the circus, eating dinner as a child with the family, talking to my surgeon father about hysterectomies and pancreatitis, playing Monopoly on Christmas Day....

The bedroom door creaked open. White light spilled into the room, blinding me momentarily and reawakening me to grim reality. A short man with a moustache entered, carefully clicked the door to, and shot the bolt. He was dressed in a green army jacket and faded jeans. Something about him made my skin crawl.

"O Lord," I thought, "if they only knew!" I raised my eyes heavenward.

The short thug walked over to my father and whispered, "Ted's ready. He'll be in in a minute." My father seemed to relax a bit.

Overhearing, I flinched. Ted? Ted Patrick! Satan Incarnate. The master sophist of the antireligion conspiracy was about to begin his task....

Again I felt panic rising inside me. Was I to be possessed as the Family had told me so many times? Would I be able to cling to God's truth? How often my spiritual father had reminded me that Satan was smarter and stronger than any ordinary man. These were the Last Days and Satan was after all of God's special children. Because I loved True Parents more than my own mother and father, because I was a prophet, because I was being trained to become a worldwide leader, Satan wanted me now more than ever.

My eyes stung as I looked around the dimly lit room at my natural father, the two gum-chewing thugs on the bed, the husky detective, and the unkempt tough guarding the door. How I wanted my spiritual parents! They'd help me if they were only here. They could defend the *Divine Principle*. They were "real pioneers," as Father called them, and I was a mere "spiritual baby," just seven months old. Satan would tear me apart for sure!

I started chanting again and felt a little better. Father had told us that if we chanted hard enough, good spirits would come to our aid. I could almost feel them. Perhaps at this very moment spirits and demons were battling it out in this dingy motel room. If only I chanted hard enough, maybe I wouldn't get possessed.

What should I do when Patrick came in? They had warned me about him: a hulking black man, a real Satan-type. They had told me he'd beat people, chain them, strip

3

them, insult Father, then brainwash his victims until they no longer believed the truth.

O Father! O Father! Father, save me!

"How ya doin', Chris?" the detective at the door asked, breaking the terrifying silence.

"Oh, great, just great." I straightened up in my chair and forced a smile, trying to look confident that I would win this bout with Satan.

The little thug with the wispy moustache snickered. He'd probably been through this a dozen times before. I had the eerie feeling that he could see right into my mind. He came over, casually sat down on the bed, leaned toward me, and peered into my eyes.

"Hey, kid, how long since ya been with a woman?"

"You know that's against my religion."

"How long ya been following your Messiah?"

I turned my head toward the wall indignantly. Nobody insults Father!

"C'mon, kid, how long? When did ya first join up?"

"Oh, about seven months ago."

"Seven and a half months," my father corrected curtly.

"You mean you haven't been with a woman for over seven months?"

Satan! Satan! Satan! I chanted to myself as I glared at my tormentor. He was attacking already!

"C'mon, kid, what could be so bad about something as nice as that?"

How could he be so disgusting? I looked down at the ground, shamed by his filthiness. If he only knew the Principle! If only he knew how he was hurting God!

All the time he had been speaking to me, the thug had never once removed the cigarette from his mouth. It was a cruel reminder of all the tobacco I had smoked in college. How often I had cried to God for forgiveness for such sin! These people were obviously determined to corrupt me. But I would remain faithful. I was a heavenly soldier, as I had sung and chanted with the Family so many hundreds of times.

In the oppressive silence, the thugs moved back and forth across the small bedroom. My father left his chair to join

the
family

one/ I awoke with a start to find myself in a strange apartment in a strange city, beautiful San Francisco. Lifting away the covers, I twisted my body out of bed. The clock on the night table read 7:15.

I drifted into the kitchen and yanked open the refrigerator door. A piece of cheese and some bread were all that remained from last night's dinner. Crumbs scraped my throat as I washed down my makeshift sandwich with gulps of instant coffee.

Time to get moving. Thoroughly awake now, I dressed and packed my bags. Suitcase in one hand, backpack securely in place, I was ready to go wherever the spirit led me in my search for answers to the overwhelming questions of the past few months. Today I planned to visit Berkeley, to explore that exciting city, where I hoped to discover the meaning of my life with all its confusions.

I clicked the apartment door to and descended into the bright new day. The morning sun was warming windy San

9

Francisco, paving the streets with fresh light. Making my way to the bus stop, I boarded the commuter's crosstown express. Ten minutes later I was in downtown San Francisco, at Powell and Market streets, where I planned to catch a subway for Berkeley. I hopped on a train, settled down in my seat, and casually glanced around me. Drops of sweat slid down my face and my well-worn jeans clung to my clammy legs, indications that I should have dressed differently for the warm June weather.

After a surprisingly short trip, the doors rolled open. I picked up my bag and stepped out. Hitching up my pack, I climbed the steps into the midst of an unfamiliar city. So this was Berkeley. It looked disappointingly like any other city. Rush-hour traffic filled the streets, crowds milled on the sidewalks, people strode briskly toward their daily tasks.

Leaning against a signpost, I unfolded a map to orient myself. Shattuck Avenue. Only three blocks to the university, and ...

"'Scuse me. My name's Jacob. You new here?"

A stocky young man with a folding table under his arm stood at my side. He seemed genuinely concerned about my confusion. I was struck by his gentle voice, the kindness in his eyes.

"I'm Chris. I just got here today."

The words were out before I knew it.

"If you need a place to stay, I'd suggest the Cal Hotel down the street."

"Oh, thanks," I said, eyeing him cautiously.

"You traveling around the country? You seem to be carrying quite a load."

It was as if he could see the sixty pounds of books stuffed in my backpack and suitcase.

"Uh, yes, I've been on the road. And you?"

"I live here in Berkeley. I spend most of my time working on community projects. I live with a group of people in town called Creative Community Projects. We're very active in the Bay Area. In fact, we run a lot of great programs to help people in Berkeley. We're a very loving, very idealistic group of young people. Say, are you interested in community living?"

"Yes, as a matter of fact, I am." I eyed him suspiciously. "Um, this group you belong to ... is it a religious group?"

"Well, not exactly. It's a social group."

"What do you mean?" I persisted. "Is it a religious group or not?"

"Well, actually yes, it *does* have a religious base," he said hesitantly. "But it includes people of all religious perspectives working together. We all feel that each religion has something special to offer. Look, why don't you join us for dinner tonight? Each evening we have an open house to welcome anyone who wants to learn about our work. Here's the address." He shoved a little white card bearing a small diagrammed street map into my hand.

"This is where you are now. Here's the hotel, and we live right here." As he traced out the way with a chubby finger, I carefully looked him over. His eyes gleamed behind Coke-bottle glasses, and he carried about 220 pounds over his six-foot frame. His stomach dripped over his belt in soft rolls of fat. His clothes were clean but shabbily tailored. Below the denim pants rested two dirty sneakers. I glanced back at his eyes, trying to size him up.

By instinct, I have always been very cautious with friendly strangers. Why ask me to dinner? I wondered. What could he possibly want? Why was he being so generous, so helpful? He didn't even know me. And what was he doing here next to the subway exit, greeting people as they entered town?

At the same time, a voice inside me whispered: Go on, Chris. Trust him. Don't be so skeptical of people. Accept the fact that there are some nice guys in the world. After all, you're searching so desperately for community. Perhaps this group has something to offer. Take a chance. Go ahead and chance a visit.

"What time is dinner?"

"You'll come? That's great, just great. Be there at six o'clock. Then we'll have time to chat before we eat. And don't forget: The Cal Hotel is that way."

I set off down the street, eager to get rid of my bag. The hotel was located above a porno theater, currently showing *Hot Rashes* three times nightly. I climbed the hotel stairs and rang a bell at the clerk's desk. A wispy little man shuffled out from a back room.

"Yes sir. Need a place to stay? How long you gonna be here?"

"At least two or three days, maybe a week."

"That'll be fine. Here's the key to room 33, young fella. It's nine dollars for tonight, prepaid. Tomorrow we can discuss rates if you decide to stay for the week."

"Okay. Thanks," I mumbled. I set off down the hall to my room, barely avoiding a lurching, wild-eyed drunk, and deposited my bag on the bare floor. I looked forward eagerly to a shower and a soft bed. After assuring myself that these comforts existed here, I left the hotel and headed toward the university.

The Berkeley campus lived up to all my California fantasies. The students looked serious and intelligent, the way I fancied myself and my fellow Yalies to be. At the same time, they looked more relaxed, less grim than their counterparts in New Haven. After a few minutes, I had found my way to the Student Center. This was familiar ground. Students were at work on the Go and chess boards. The usual collection of pipe-smoking philosophers and to-be lawyers rubbed shoulders with Frisbee-playing hippies and their dogs and engineering students equipped with their mechanical-pencil collections. The room was silent except for the rustle of *Berkeley Barbs* and *Wall Street Journals*, the click-click of pocket calculators, the earnest hushed conversations over chains of cigarettes and cups of lukewarm coffee.

I glanced at the bulletin boards assigned to student-activity announcements. Most of the articles advertised methods of self-help or spiritual paths of liberation. More than the usual crowd of self-realized masters were advertising for followers. Side by side were plastered ads for psycho-synthesis, kundalini yoga, TM, Rolffing, women's consciousness centers, and speed reading. Each group had a service to offer.

In the lower corner of the bulletin board I spotted an ad for Creative Community Projects. Penciled in above a few simplistic lines about peace and happiness was a sun and a smiley face. Oh, God! What was I in for? Would they turn out to be just a bunch of happy idiots from overprotected homes who wanted to be friendly? Or was there a catch? Could they be selling something?

I unstrapped my backpack, eased into a sagging chair, and yawned. The strain of the last four years had taken its toll in ways no one knew. Four years of grinding and searching at Yale; four years of trying to carve a place for myself in an immensely complex society. Four years of increasing disillusionment as I saw my utopian dreams and intellectual castles come tumbling down...

I remembered moving into my freshman dorm at Yale in the fall of 1971, unpacking my boxes, eager for a four-year adventure, an intellectual feast. Just turned seventeen, I was fresh from a small suburban prep school, secure in my love of learning, certain that I would emerge from college with the knowledge and commitment to do something worthwhile with my life.

But my youthful illusions were short-lived. Having weathered the spurt of idealistic enthusiasm of the sixties, Yale, like other institutions of its kind, was busily manufacturing doctors, lawyers, politicians, and businessmen primed to control the offices of Wall Street, Madison Avenue, and the bureaucracies of Washington, the exclusive country clubs and corporate conglomerates throughout the country. I quickly vowed to myself not to follow in the path of the grim-eyed seniors whom I saw as selling out for a handsome price.

As my fears of compromise heightened, I saw what had begun as an adolescent community fragment into cliques as my classmates picked their fields of study and appropriate alliances. When not competing for grades, girl friends, and political power on campus, my friends and roommates would spend hours over the dinner table trying to act more clever, more sophisticated than their uneasy allies and companions. Night after night I watched them play their petty, destructive games, their verbal jousts, their endless mocking and scorning. I acted out in turn, halfheartedly conforming to various campus stereotypes—jock, hippie, intellectual—until I realized that the masks were becoming more and more difficult to remove....

In an attempt to survive without the easy acceptance I had dreamed of, I gradually withdrew into myself, seeking self-knowledge through the study of psychology and philosophy. As my isolation increased, I began to people my world with intellectual heroes, long-dead misanthropes, and guiding geniuses whom I strove to emulate: Aristotle, Kant, Husserl, and above all Hegel. Abandoning all hope for the loveless society in which I found myself, I retreated into the world of the mind for the answers I sought, hoping to publish eventually in erudite journals. Time and again I considered dropping out of the undergraduate maze to find "education" elsewhere, but my insatiable commitment to learning and the need to associate with professors involved in its pursuit kept me anchored....

Then halfway through my senior year, something snapped. Suddenly I saw the intellectual life I was pursuing as one more grand illusion. My professors, it seemed to me, were shaping my thoughts, not expanding them. Their main commitment was to tenure and to their self-images as mentors, not to knowledge. All my gods had finally fallen, casting me adrift in a world without love or direction.

It was then, shortly before graduation, that I sought a knowledge that was pure, a knowledge based on love, a knowledge that I hoped would bridge the gulf between science and religion. It was then that I turned my gaze toward the heavens....

God seemed my only hope, my sole chance. I had never considered God seriously except as an abstract and unprovable concept. I had rarely attended church since I left Sunday school after growing tired of tracing my hands on paper with crayons and writing, "These are the hands of Jesus." Most religious people I knew seemed loving, yet surprisingly innocent and unable to justify their faith to me. But one spring night, sitting in my room, writing a senior paper on developmental psychology, my body was gripped by waves of fear as I suddenly realized that perhaps the true, the ultimate answers to life I was seeking must come from beyond the intellect. Perhaps knowledge was not to be discovered but received. I considered the words of Jesus: "Ask and it shall be given to you; seek and ye shall find." And so with everything to gain and nothing to lose, I fell to my knees and begged:

"Lord, if ever there is, if ever there was, a Creator, if there exists a being great enough to love me, to answer my questions, to give me my life—O God, O God, if you are out there and if you care, touch me—touch me, please!"

Suddenly, just as suddenly as they had begun, the waves disappeared and I found myself at peace. Astonished, I asked: "O Lord, are you really there, or is this some sort of supreme joke?"

The crown of my head began to tingle. Streams of love—for lack of a better word—began flowing through my body like a mysterious current of bliss. I was overcome with joy.

Now, sitting here in my armchair at Berkeley, I could almost relive my excitement. And I recalled how that night I had prayed ever so awkwardly and continued praying each day for weeks, praying for the simplest things, but praying above all for some sort of self-understanding. Within a few days I began meeting people of various faiths in New Haven who engaged in long conversations with me about God. I listened intently, praying that somehow God was speaking through them. I started seriously reading the Bible, seeking the love and wisdom of God through the words of the prophets. I was prepared to do anything to shed my past fears and misunderstandings and enjoy direct communication with that being for which thousands of sages, saints, gurus, and rabbis had lived and died. I was determined to search, to go anywhere to achieve such transcendence. And I desperately hoped that, if there was a God of love, there were others like myself with whom I could share my desires. Perhaps somewhere out there was a community where I would be free to love and learn and where I would be loved and taught, as I had wanted so much at college and so sadly missed.

I fingered the card Jacob had given me, turned it over, glanced back at the bulletin board across from me. Scrawny little Indian men with beady eyes stared back, a pubescent fat guru offered divine knowledge, mimeographed saviors sweated blood and offered outstretched hands. I smiled to myself, for I was clearly not alone in my search for God! I had heard that Berkeley was a sort of seeker's paradise, a place where holy men of all faiths resided and young people flocked to find themselves. Judging from the array of advertisements and posters proliferating in the city, it must be so. And since this was also the residence of several brilliant theorists in physics and metaphysics, the three-thousand-mile journey from Connecticut should prove to be well worth my while.

I pulled an apple out of my backpack and polished it carefully on my checkered shirt. As I munched away, I wondered why spirituality was on the rise in this country, why thousands of young people were delving into the occult, chanting, meditating, dancing in the streets. Within a few short years, the "counterculture" had moved from politics to acid, from acid to Eastern spirituality. Harvard professors and New York psychologists were returning from India with enticing stories of Eastern knowledge. Well-educated young men and women, tired of neurotic parents and peers, boring pot parties, and the maze-running of American college education were eagerly swallowing candy-sweet promises of inner bliss. Was theirs the ultimate retreat from the overwhelming problems of a crumbling society, or was God calling all his children home?

Finishing my apple, aiming at the wastebasket, firing the core, and—pow—making a basket, I wondered if there might be some truth within the barrage of Eastern consciousness rhetoric. Was I destined to become yet another guru-junkie, following some saffron-robed Tibetan peasant through his spacious Berkeley ashram, hoping that he would touch my forehead with his magic holy feather and bless me? Was I to chant with the Hare Krishnas, dress dolls in elaborate clothing and drink cow urine in secret ritual each morning, smear my forehead with holy cow dung and dream of those most sacred creatures aimlessly chewing their cuds while Indian children starved in the streets? Was there no end to the desperation of my brothers and sisters of this country? And was I not equally disillusioned and desperate in my own way, as I began to believe that I might not arrive at truth through the power of thought alone, that I might be forced to rely on a revelation or mystical experience of God given to me or somebody else? I had no more absolute values, no way to judge right and wrong. Perhaps I should only trust God, place my faith—what a queer and mysterious word, *faith*—in God and hope He or It would somehow deliver. ...

Would I regret leaving my sad and confused parents shortly after graduation, telling them to give away all my possessions, warning them that I wouldn't be seeing them for a long, long time—perhaps never? Could they possibly imagine the fever for God burning within my heart, those nominal Christians of my neighborhood who stepped into churches only for occasional weddings, funerals, and the traditional Christmas services?

As I mused, a beautiful, braless co-ed sauntered by, a copy of Balzac tucked under her arm. A wonderful California woman, so different from her tense eastern counterparts. I smiled. She smiled, tossed her sun-bleached hair across her shoulders, and continued on her way, obviously enjoying the attention. I thought of the broken relationships I had had at Yale, especially my last one with Karen. I saddened as I recalled how that relationship was destroyed as my intellectual bubbles were pricked. I had turned inward and she had turned to an Iraqi Marxist. And so I had left Yale brokenhearted.

I must have dozed off for a while—these last weeks were taking their toll. Jumping to my feet, I threw my pack on my back and glanced at my watch. Six o'clock. Grabbing my things, I pushed my way past undergraduates to the door and hurried across campus, following Jacob's directions. A free meal and a chance to meet some friendly people certainly sounded appealing. I hoped they could direct me to people who could help me answer my questions and continue my spiritual pursuits.

I didn't know what to expect as I climbed the hill and headed up Hearst Street, following the route on the card. Perhaps this was one of those Christian fellowship groups that were springing up throughout the country. There it was, an impressive mansion at the top of the hill. No, that couldn't be right. The house looked much too lavish. But this *was* the address Jacob had given me. I continued up the well-tended walk, climbed the front steps, and cautiously opened the imposing front door.

Before me stretched an immense hallway echoing with the sound of youthful voices. Young men and women were walking around in their socks. Lines of shoes stood like soldiers at the front door. I stripped off my pack and work boots and looked about uneasily.

"Oh, hi, there! What's youuuuuuur name?" a fresh-faced young woman trilled, hurrying up to greet me. She beamed at me with the simple delighted look of a small child.

"I'm Chris," I said quietly.

"Welllllll, don't just stand there. Come in!" Her theatrics embarrassed me. Why was she so glad to see me? Stop it Chris, I told myself firmly, you're just being skeptical, as usual. You think so little of yourself that you wonder why anyone else would care. Go ahead. Go on inside and join them. What have you got to lose?

Leaving my belongings at the door, I started down the carpeted hallway. Everyone I passed swung around, grabbed my hand, and shook it warmly. At the same time, they looked me straight in the eyes and said something personal like: "Hi, I'm Nancy. Say, that's such a cute shirt you're wearing." In spite of their friendliness, there was something about those smiling faces that bothered me. Their eyes, that was it. They all had glassy eyes, like two eggs sunny side up, open so wide that the pupils seemed to bulge out of their faces. . . .

The Family

I entered a large room at the end of the hall which was filled with neatly dressed young people in their twenties, all sitting on the floor in circles. Each person had a plate of vegetables in front of him or her. They were speaking in quiet voices with a lot of smiling and laughing. I spotted about fifteen other bewildered-looking people in the group, obviously guests like myself, being entertained by their hosts. In spite of the movement and chatter, the atmosphere in the crowded room seemed remarkably calm and curiously controlled.

A young woman in a prim, flower-print dress approached me.

"You must be Jacob's guest! Come right in, sit down over here. Let me get you some dinner. Gee, you look tired. Have you had a long journey?"

Before I could answer, she had disappeared. By the time she returned with a plateful of salad and broccoli, I had struck up a conversation with some of the other people in the circle in which she had placed me.

"You must be Chris. Jacob said you'd be coming. I'm Janis, and this is my guest, Bill. We met today down on the campus. You met Jacob down on Shattuck, didn't you?"

I nodded. How did she know?

"Excuse me a minute, Chris. I think Jacob's arrived. Let me get him. Meanwhile, you and Bill can get acquainted."

Bill was a sickly-looking young man with a disoriented, spaced-out look. He told me that he had been hitchhiking around the country for quite some time now, ever since dropping out of Memphis State. He was planning to leave Berkeley for the East Coast, and from there go on to India, where he hoped to find a spiritual leader. I noticed that both he and Janis had crusty deposits on either side of their mouths, which I knew was a sign of vitamin deficiency.

As Bill talked on, I sensed that, like so many other sons and daughters of the middle class, he was disgusted with the very values that had created him and was searching desperately for something greater than himself, seeking a spiritual alternative to the rampant materialism that permeated the "free world." Three years of searching for true values in a throwaway world had left him exhausted, desperate for the basic support that only accepting peers can give. Where would his journey lead him? I wondered.

Janis came scurrying back with Jacob. My host seemed to be quite a celebrity here, for people kept coming up to him and shaking his hand. He greeted me with a smile:

"Hi, Chris! Thanks for coming tonight. I hope you'll stay for a short lecture after dinner. It'll tell you all about what we do in the Family."

The Family? So that's what they called themselves ...

I spent the next half hour talking to the people in my circle. They seemed to hang onto every word I said, acting terribly interested in whatever I mentioned. They asked me what I had studied in school, what I was doing in California, and what my interests were. Before long some of them were questioning me more deeply, asking whether I had any religious background. But they changed the subject quickly when they saw that this was a touchy issue.

I asked them several questions about their community but they seemed to hedge each time.

"What's life like in this Family of yours?" I asked a red-cheeked young man.

"Great, just great!"

"Do you all live together in some sort of commune arrangement?"

"Well, it's *like* a commune—actually more like a—a spiritual community of sorts."

"A monastery?" I chuckled.

"No, no—we're just a group of concerned people trying to lead conscientious, loving lives. We're really improving ourselves."

"How many people live in this house. It's pretty large, pretty expensive-looking. You must need eight or ten to pay the rent."

"Oh, yes, more than eight or ten."

"How many?"

"Well, between thirty-five and forty ... "

"What?"

"Well, it's not always that many. We move around a lot and ... "

"Forty people? Men and women together?"

"Well, on separate floors, of course."

"With all those people what about sexual relationships? Don't things get a bit—complex?"

"Uh, we have high spiritual standards here."

"You didn't answer my question."

"Oh, we believe there's a time and a place for everything. Just listen to the lectures after dinner. They'll tell you everything."

He picked up his plate and headed for the broccoli.

As I chatted with the other members of the circle, I noticed a peculiar pattern emerging from the group. After asking me a personal question, Family members would respond to my answer by saying how much their situation was like mine. They seemed to be playing upon my identity, deliberately trying to draw me close. I resented this intrusion on a life that was uniquely mine, but I felt more bewildered than resentful. Just what were they up to?

After about twenty minutes, Jacob returned my empty plate to the serving table and announced that the evening's entertainment was about to begin. Suddenly folding chairs appeared from nowhere and the room was quickly converted into a lecture hall by scurrying youths. The program began with the singing of children's songs, and favorite hit love songs. The male group members dressed in ties and jackets and the Family women in pleated skirts entered into the singing with tremendous enthusiasm, while most of the guests, like myself, sat silently and watched. There was something about the entertainment that seemed very carefully orchestrated, even the way the well-scrubbed audience was clapping riotously to the music.

As I clapped politely along to the singing, I looked around me. The contrast between the scraggly newcomers and the thirty or forty cherry-cheeked all-American regulars was striking. The people here seemed so straight, or at least those who appeared to be part of the Family. The women, like

21

the men, had extremely short hair. They all had large, dark circles under their eyes, yet they radiated the energy of Romper Room kiddies. Between songs they giggled, held hands, or stared at their fellow Family members who gathered at the mike as the host called them from the audience to sing. It was all sweetness and light, like a Georgia tent revival being staged in one of the most sophisticated cities in the nation. I felt as though I had been catapulted back in time. Everything here seemed so old-fashioned, from the choice of songs to the clothes, to the stilted language the Family used. Yet despite myself, I enjoyed the sense of innocence, so different from the Yalie Sherry Hour and cocktail party hype which I despised so much.

After about twenty minutes of singing, the host of the evening introduced the president of the group, Dr. Irving Dust. A short, meticulously dressed man immediately came to the front of the room and launched into a polished monologue with the smoothness of a pro. As he mouthed a string of unconnected but common truths, such as "Everybody wants to get together, but we just can't do it alone," or "The world is crying out for more love," he waved a series of cardboard posters at the audience. Most of the lecture struck me as sheer rhetoric, with little if any structure.

"Why do we let arrogance blind us to the truth?" Dust demanded. "Why are we skeptical?" Holding up a drawing of an elephant, he launched into the fable about three blindmen trying to describe the mammoth despite their limited point of view. He emphasized that we all have a part of The Truth, but we must get together and see the whole picture.

Jacob, seated at my side, urged me to pay close attention to the lecture. Each time I turned to speak to him, he told me to observe Dr. Dust closely. There was something hypnotic about the little man's smooth, rhythmic delivery. As I watched him, my mind seemed to drift away ... I tuned in again whenever he offhandedly mentioned his experience as a psychotherapist, his conversation with Nobel Prize-winning physicists, his work with the popular humanist Abraham Maslow, and the marvelous ideals of the Family.

The Family

The lecture finally ended, to my relief. Family members clapped wildly as Dust proceeded down the aisle in his Hickey-Freeman suit. The audience stood up as if on cue, and Family members led their guests into the next room for tea and cookies. Three smiling young men, one of whom introduced himself as Mitch, surrounded me immediately and asked how I'd liked the talk. I told them how refreshing I found the Family's innocence, enthusiasm, and openness.

"Yes, and we have *great* times together, Chris," Mitch replied. "Since you enjoyed this evening so much, why don't you join us this weekend? We've planned a great trip—out to the country to a place called Boonville. You'll just love it there. Do you like animals? We have all sorts of animals on the Farm. We play games like volleyball together, we swim together, and we sing together all weekend. I know you'll be glad you came."

A trip to the country *did* sound tempting.

"Well, I don't have anything special planned for this weekend, uh ... "

"Great! Just great! We're going to have so much fun. We can pick up your bag on the way. We ride to the Farm in a big old school bus, singing our hearts out. It's just great that you're coming, Chris!"

Now that I had agreed, Mitch and his friends turned to a guest behind me and began trying to convince him also to join in the weekend excursion.

Why were these people so eager to spend a weekend with total strangers? I wondered. Although I had no real evidence, I was suspicious that there was some sort of surprise in store for me. But I was eager for diversion, a little adventure. And if their philosophy didn't make sense or things didn't work out, I could always leave ... couldn't I?

Soon after dark, we trooped outside and piled into a yellow school bus painted with elephant faces on the side. Mitch sat down beside me, explaining that he would be acting as my host for the weekend. We sang jolly songs and socialized all the way up to the Farm. But the songs were different from those sung at dinner. Many of them referred to the Family: how great it was, how desperate everyone had been before he joined the group, how wonderful group life was. Some of the songs were explicitly religious, in spite of the fact that God had been mentioned only once—in passing—in Dr. Dust's lecture. I sensed a change in the atmosphere, a new proselytizing note. People kept coming up the aisle to shake my hand. Before the trip was over, I had met at least thirty people, all of whom acted as though I was their long-lost brother.

We arrived at the farm encampment about midnight. The headlights of the Elephant Bus flashed on a neatly lettered sign:

PLEASE DO NOT ENTER WITHOUT PRIOR PERMISSION OF OWNER UNDER PENALTY OF LAW

As the driver beeped the horn, a guard dressed in jeans and a workshirt appeared to unlock the barbed-wire gate and wave us in. As the bus passed through, I wondered why out in the middle of nowhere, a farm would have fences, gates, and guards....

We spilled out of the bus, forded a tiny brook, and walked through a field toward a large, dingy structure which a Family member told me was called the Chicken Palace. A former hen house, it had been converted into a dormitory and lecture hall. The women left us here and went on to a nearby trailer which served as their sleeping quarters. We wearily spread out sleeping bags on the bare floor, as instructed, and one Family member told us to go to sleep immediately. Before closing my eyes, I glanced over at Mitch. He was down on his hands and knees, deep in prayer.

two/ "Good morning, brothers!"

At around 7:30 A.M. three rosy-cheeked men burst into the Chicken Palace, twanging away on guitars. As they sang "Morning Is Broken," Family members popped out of their sleeping bags. Where did they get their energy, I wondered, as I struggled out of my slumber.

Mitch reached down and extended his hand to me. Pulling me out of my bag, he dusted me off and beamed at me paternally. I was completely taken aback by his fatherly gesture. What right did he have to treat me like a son on a camp outing?

As I tried to get my bearings, a sandy-haired youth bounced up, slapped me on the back, pumped my hand, and shouted in my ear, "Good morning, brother. My name's Jackie." When Mitch explained to him that Jacob was my "spiritual father," Jackie looked at me with awe.

"What's a spiritual father?" I asked.

"That's what you call the person who brings you to the Family. But you'll learn more about that later. I'll tell you this, though. You're very lucky, Chris," Jackie confided. Bending his head toward Mitch, I heard him whisper, "He must be very close to Heavenly Father." Just what did he mean by that? I was beginning to suspect that a lot of information was being withheld from me. But before I could ask further questions, Mitch grabbed me by the hand and pulled me outside.

"Exercise time!" he shouted. One hundred fifty people had suddenly gathered from nowhere into one large circle and were doing toe touches and jumping jacks. The leader reminded me of the head of a kindergarten class. He used cutesy language to describe each exercise, squealing with enjoyment as the group did push-ups and clowning around as he told us to jump up and reach the sky. He next instructed us to all hold hands and join in the circle to sing songs of innocence.

When the singing was over the leader shouted:

"How 'bout a choo-choo?"

"Yay, yay!" people scattered through the ring shouted back. Family members squeezed the hands of bewildered guests, pumped the hands up and down, and jumped in rhythm to screams of:

"*Choo-choo-choo, choo-choo-choo, choo-choo-choo. Yay, yay—Pow!*"

Two smiling people shook and jostled me through this mystifying ritual. As I attempted to recover my balance, Jacob appeared, waved to me, and began reading names off a list.

"The following people are in Edie's group: Bill Mantle, Walter Ashe, Susan Greenwald ... "

We each found the groups to which we were assigned, scurrying around like children inside the circle. I was in Jacob's group, along with Jackie and Mitch and five other Family members and guests. Breakfast was served on the lawn, chocolate milk and granola in Styrofoam cups. While we ate, various group members talked about their lives in an easy, relaxed way. As I looked around the circle of smiling faces, I began to feel a strange sense of kinship with this Family.

After we'd emptied our cups, Jacob told us it was time to attend a lecture in the Chicken Palace. We filed into the ramshackle structure, received songbooks, and headed for the rows of metal chairs. The music had already begun, a frenetic rousing song telling us how important this moment was for us.

"These are the Last Days, yes, these are the Last Days!" the Family chanted. The message was obvious. We were assembled to hear the Word of God. The singing lasted twenty minutes, with much clapping and riotous shouting. The song leader, a pink-faced woman in her thirties, got so carried away she snapped a guitar string in her fervor. Undaunted, she picked up the spare guitar at her side and continued.

The supercharged atmosphere and the Family's wild enthusiasm left me bewildered and disoriented. Like the other guests, I was surrounded by group members who kept urging me to clap and sing. The music suddenly picked up in tempo:

Oh, Glo-ri-ous E-den, garden of delight!
In the beauty of Cre-a-tion let us all re-joice!

The music surged. Every few bars the men stood up and the women promptly sat down. Then the men plopped down and the women popped up. I couldn't seem to keep up, to find a pattern to this frenzy. In my confusion I abandoned myself to the leadership of the group members around me. Whenever it was time for me to stand up, they grabbed me by the arms and pulled me up. As I was just about to balance myself on my feet, they pushed me back down into the chair, manipulating me like a puppet.

The group ran through an entire repertoire of songs, each one sillier than the next. These were interspersed with religious songs proclaiming some sort of new Messiah:

Oh the Lord is come...
Crushing the forces of sin...
He dispels the dark night...
Accept the Lord ... Here is the King of Kings.

Flipping through my song book, I noticed that it was divided into sections, with familiar favorites first, followed by religious songs, followed by curious selections written in a totally unfamiliar tongue. As I puzzled over these unintelligible verses, the group burst into a fast-moving song which referred to something called True Parents:

> *New cul-ture dawns in the East...*
> *Mankind trans-formed in its light shall be one fam-i-ly.*
> *Ever to serve and at-tend our True Parents' own...*
> *We're his pride in the heav-en-ly war...*

The songs moved too fast and were too vague in meaning to do anything but bewilder me. I tried to be polite and to sing along, looking to the members for help. They were quick to respond, leading me like a child.

"Just keep singing, Chris," Mitch encouraged me. "Later you'll understand."

As I joined in with the others, a Family member who had been introduced to me as Eileen whispered, "You're such a lucky heavenly child to have Jacob as your parent. He's just won-derful!"

Parent? Heavenly child? What was she talking about? I wasn't part of this so-called Family. I was just a weekend guest. What were these people up to?

Eileen must have sensed my annoyance. She took my hand and slapped it.

"Now, don't be negative, Chris! Try to smile and have a good time. You'll understand everything after you hear the lectures."

I shrugged and continued singing. After a few minutes, Dr. Dust appeared at the front of the room carrying a familiar-looking pile of cardboard posters which he placed on an easel. The music quickly died down. As Dust began speaking, I recognized the identical lecture of the night before!

"What's going on?" I grumbled to Eileen.

"Now, you just be quiet and respect Dr. Dust. He's our leader here. Besides, there's so much packed into each lecture, you can hear it over and over. I've heard this one at least fifty times and I still learn from it."

Dr. Dust held up the large elephant cartoon.

"Why are we skeptical?" he asked. The audience responded in unison.

"Because of our own partial viewpoint!" Titters in the background. Not again! Did Dust plan to repeat that stupid story about the elephant and the three blind men? Yet in spite of Dust's familiar rhetoric, I began to listen more closely than the previous evening, drawn by the rhythm in his gestures, the soft, seductive sound of his voice.

Once again Dust's theme was that we are so arrogant that we may not recognize the Truth when we hear it. The implication, of course, was that the "Truth" was being told to us here, in this lecture, and we must be humble enough to listen. Garbage, I thought. Yet I longed so deeply for Community ... I desired so much to realize my hopes and goals in a communal framework ... I wanted so badly to believe. And, stupid as the lectures sounded, there was little with which I could really disagree. As I looked around, I saw smiling faces nodding in agreement at their bald, bespectacled leader. What made them look so happy? What was their secret? Was there something at the heart of this talk that I was missing?

The lecture ended with a roar of applause, an irresistible tide of enthusiasm. It was followed by a song of celebration, then a prayer. A prayer? No one had mentioned praying!

"Dear Heavenly Father, we thank You so much for being with us today, for guiding our guests here. We hope and pray we can be faithful to Your good will."

God's will? If God's will was so important to the Family, why hadn't they told me that they were a religious community in the first place? I turned to Jacob accusingly, but before I could voice my objections, he grabbed my hand and led me outside.

We reassembled by groups on the lawn near the Chicken Palace. Jacob explained that we would now discuss the lecture.

"Jackie, what inspirations did you get from Dr. Dust's talk?"

Jackie started things off by confessing his arrogance and explaining how Dr. Dust had made him understand how the sin of pride had blinded him to the Truth. Jacob then turned to me. When I explained that I hadn't been impressed by the lecture, he immediately called on another Family member, who announced:

"The first time I heard the lectures I wasn't impressed either. But that's because I wouldn't open my heart to God. Now that I'm in the Family, I feel so much closer to God. God can speak in the lectures through Dr. Dust, who is so very close to Him. Thank Heavenly Father that I'm here to hear the Truth."

Each such confession was accompanied by clapping and backslapping. I was beginning to get the message: If you didn't agree with the Family, something was clearly wrong with you.

Shortly after the confessional ended, we were herded back to the Chicken Palace. Another lecture faced us, this one explicitly talking about God for the first time. Dust stressed what he called the "Principle of Creation," basically a modern Christianlike account of God's presence in nature. Again his talk was preceded and followed by singing—frantic, excited singing. The noise and emotion drained me, clouded my thinking, kept me from concentrating on Dust's words. In the discussion period that followed, I noticed that any questions that could be answered were easily dealt with, but the more difficult or unanswerable questions were bypassed, with Jacob simply saying that if we waited until the lectures were over, Dust's meaning would become clear.

"Just have patience," he insisted. Perhaps he was right. In any case, rather than question now, it was all I could do to keep my integrity intact amid the emotional bombardment which seemed to be steadily increasing....

After a quick lunch on the lawn, Family members jumped to their feet, took their guests by the hands, and led them to a nearby field to play dodge ball. As I kicked at the ground, sending up clouds of dust, I savored schoolboy pleasures revisited. I looked around at the usual sea of smiling faces. But now deep in the Family members' eyes I glimpsed a chilling single-mindedness, an intent that both bewildered and fascinated me. What lay behind this supposedly innocent game?

Each group divided up into one of two teams. Each team was appointed a captain who suggested a cheer and team chant. During the entire game our team chanted loudly, "Bomb with Love," "Blast with Love," as the soft, round balls volleyed back and forth. Again I felt lost and confused, angry, remote and helpless, for the game had started without an explanation of the rules. The guests were being moved around the field like robots on roller skates.

"Listen, Chris," Jacob called from the sidelines. "If you don't understand the rules, just chant or cheer as loudly as possible. The important thing is to do whatever a Family member tells you. Remember, unity is everything here."

I dutifully started shouting.

"Louder, louder, Chris. That's it. Just follow me." He placed me in a new position and I clapped mechanically. A few minutes later, he moved me again.

I noticed how aggressively the Family members played, how they constantly eyed their guests, coaxing them to chant out loud. As I clapped and shouted, I could feel my tension slipping away, my sense of involvement growing. In spite of myself, I felt a desire to merge into this Family, this group, this game, to become a part of this vibrant, loving circle. "Give in, Chris," urged a voice within me. "Just be a child and obey. It's fun. It's trusting. Isn't this the innocence, the purity of love, you've been searching for?"

The game ended before I had figured out the rules.

"C'mon, Chris. Let's go. Another exciting lecture!" Jacob shouted as he took my hand and yanked.

We trotted off in a line to the Chicken Palace for another singing session of twenty minutes which we were told was designed to prepare us spiritually for the next talk, a lecture on guiding ideals and historical failures. In another droning monologue, Dr. Dust tried to show how history had led us to a climactic point, the New Age, in which we were living now.

When Dust had completed his third talk of the day, we reassembled in groups for dinner. As we ate, Family members praised the lecture and goaded their guests to do the same. I noticed that there was not enough food to go around. The same had been true at lunch, and tonight, like then, Jacob took part of his meal and gave it to me with a loving smile.

"Please take my dinner, Chris. I don't want it anyway," he insisted. I was touched at the way he took his own food and gave it to me. He wasn't the only one. As dirty fingers worked busily around the circle, I suddenly found mounds of peanut-butter cookies sitting before me. Smiley faces beamed back at me in response to my look of surprise. Simple. Childish, of course. But the Family's sincerity touched me once again. I gobbled a few cookies, then pushed the rest into the center of the circle, while Family members sang praises to life in the group.

After we finished dinner, Jacob told us that each weekend group traditionally made up a song or skit to present to the entire audience. The leaders usually wrote most of the song, but guests were expected to contribute something as well. As our group supervisor, Jacob asked me to write a line or two describing how lonely life had been before I heard the Truth and joined the Family. I noticed that other guests were being prodded to declare themselves as well, to write and sing things that they seemed reluctant to express and may not have even believed. Jacob teased and goaded and finally ordered me to commit myself, badgering me until I finally gave in. He seemed delighted with the few lines I unwillingly scrawled about how happy everyone at Boonville seemed. Beaming, he led us back into the Chicken Palace, now buzzing with activity as young men and women streamed in from around the Farm.

Show time! We sat on the floor like little children as the first group gathered in front of the audience. Along with the other guests, I observed silently while the supervisors tittered and jostled each other like five-year-olds. Two giggling Family members in the corner were playing patty-cake....

The Family

The first performance looked like the work of a pack of overgrown Cub Scouts. Complete with makeup and funny hats, backpacks and umbrellas, the players poked fun at the searching so many of them had experienced before joining the Family. I was amazed at how readily the guests were participating. They all sang the last verse together, a tribute to Heavenly Father, thanking Him for guiding them here. All the skits of the evening were similar, carefully guided by the supervisors, dwelling on the same themes of infinite despair and hope. I noticed that even the most callous guest eventually responded after being tickled, mocked, poked, or otherwise treated as a naughty little child by his supervisor, until he or she complied out of sheer embarrassment.

Ours was the last group to perform. I reluctantly joined in as we sang about how we had all found God's love and true happiness here on the Farm. After we finished our song and dance, the crowd cheered riotously, not for us but for Dr. Dust, who had suddenly appeared on stage for a little entertainment of his own. He seemed bursting with fatherly love for this roomful of overgrown children. As a good-night treat, he offered a raspy rendition of his generation's favorite, "Only for You." The young women swooned and held their hands to their hearts, much to Dust's obvious delight. When he finished, the crowd screamed and cheered like boisterous kiddies of the famous Peanut Gallery on the *Howdy Doody Show*.

The evening ended with hot chocolate and marshmallows, my boyhood favorite. After munching and chatting for a few minutes, I ducked out to go to the bathroom. Jackie and Mitch were immediately at my heels. While I stood in the stall for my nocturnal, Jackie chatted nonstop through the door. With a shiver, I realized that the Family had not left me alone for a single moment since my arrival on the farm.... .

As I arranged my sleeping bag on the floor of the Chicken Palace, Jackie and Mitch stretched their own bags out beside me. In the group breakfast, I had been told that we three should "stick together like peanut-butter sandwiches," but weren't they overdoing it? I zipped up with a sigh. Before falling asleep, I looked over at Mitch and Jackie. Encased in their sleeping bags, they were squatting on their knees like a pair of mantises. For the next twenty minutes they prayed softly:

> *Oooooo please oooooo please my Heavenly Father. My dearest Heavenly Father, ooooopleaseooopleaselisten to me. Father, Heavenly Father, thankYousomuch for this marvelous opportunity to serveYou. ThankYousomuch for the bugs and the bees and the birdsthatfly through the air. ThankYousomuch for saving me from certain death. ThankYousoverymuch for bringing me to the Family. Oooooopleaseooooplease protect Father on this earth. Thank You for sending us another son. We pray that we won't butcherhim like your last son. OGODmyFather, dearest Heavenly Father, please be with us this day. Please protect ChrisandMichelleandEveyandJacobandSally and our whole group of heavenly children. Here we are nested together like bugsinarug. We hope we can all hear Your message from our Abba, Dr. Dust. Pleasework through Dr. Dust and wellgee, please work through all of us. Pleaseforgiveme for being so impure, forgive me for my nastythoughtstoday.*
> (Pause)
> *SATAN-GET-OUT! SATANGETOUT!!! In Master's Name, Satan get out!!!*
> (Pause)
> *OooooHeavenlyFather I am so-oooo impure! DearHeavenly FATHER please forgive me for my sins today. Strike me down, make me ill to pay indemnity for this.*
> *PleasebringChris to the Family heissorighteousandpure and forgivehim for his sins. Please open his spiritual eyes and ears to hear Your message and protect him from SATAN! In Master'sName I pray, aaaaaa-men.*

three/ "C'mon, Chris. You're taking too

much time. We'll miss out on all the fun. We've got a busy
schedule today."

Jacob pulled me away from the sink where I was sleepily
splashing water on my face. Leading me by the hand, he
hurried me out into the crisp morning air. All around us,
supervisors were busily lining up guests on the lawn.

As I took my place in Jacob's exercise circle, I noticed that
Frank, one of the other guests in Jacob's group, was missing. I
asked Jacob where he was.

"Oh, Frank was negative. We decided he better not stay
in the group, so we told him to leave early this morning." I
shrugged my shoulders. Perhaps he couldn't stand the
pressure for conversion. I wondered how many other guests
had been quietly ushered out during the night and dropped
on a remote country road near this God-knows-where Farm.

After morning exercises, we broke up into our small
groups for breakfast. I found five bowls of granola piled up at
my place. . . .

"Time to share daily goals," Jacob announced brightly. "It's one of the ways we become more loving within our loving Family. Why don't you go first, Mitch?"

"I want to come closer to Heavenly Father by taking his viewpoint in every situation. He has been suffering for six thousand years. I want to have Father's compassion today. I also plan to listen closely to each lecture, to hear Heavenly Father work through Dr. Dust."

I was astonished by these goals. Twenty-four hours ago I had no idea that this was a religious group. Now I was being asked to focus my thoughts on a "Heavenly Father" I didn't even know. On the one hand, I wanted to conform to the group's expectations and plan righteous goals to please them. On the other, I didn't want to be insincere to myself or anyone else. I decided I would plan modest goals when Jacob called on me.

"I want to listen closely to the lectures and determine whether they're true," I announced when my turn came.

Two of the supervisors looked at me condescendingly. I felt like shouting: How can you be so goddamn self-righteous? What makes you think you can dictate my thoughts and emotions? How can you sit in the middle of a California farm, pledge your life to God, and expect direct guidance? And how can you ask it of me? But I refrained out of politeness to my hosts.

Jacob responded instantly.

"That's just great, Chris. Listen closely. There's plenty more to come."

He quickly pressed on, calling on the other group members to share their confessions and plans. After he had gone around the circle he abruptly rose to his feet.

"Time for morning lecture."

Family members responded on cue, collecting their guests and trotting over a bridge to the Chicken Palace for twenty minutes of intense prelecture singing. When Dr. Dust entered the room, he received a standing ovation. Jacob pulled me up and out of my seat.

"C'mon, be respectful to Dr. Dust. We're so lucky to have such heavenly guidance here."

As the lecture began, I noticed Family members bow their heads in prayer. In spite of the lecture's apparent importance, I was surprised to see an astounding number of them begin nodding off. As each person fell asleep, someone nearby would rap him hard on the forehead, awakening him with a start. This seemed to be a very sleepy flock of heavenly children.

I wondered what caused such exhaustion. As I sat watching, a number of the dozers stood up and walked up to the back of the hall. Soon, there were twenty or more Family members, shuffling from foot to foot, trying to keep awake.

Dr. Dust was in full voice at the front of the lecture hall, weaving artful phrases as he discussed man's need for guilt in abandoning God. He declared Jesus Christ to be a martyr for our sins. If only we had all followed Jesus during his life, we could have sinless lives for this world and the next, he claimed.

"Jesus was not meant to die," Dust shouted. "He died because of our failures. We let God down; we bypassed the chance for salvation of the world. What was the goal of Jesus? Simply, to establish the Kingdom of Heaven on Earth. What did he teach us? The same message of all prophets: Love others as you love yourself. When Buddha left his kingly estate for a life of meditation, he spent seven years wondering just what was the root of suffering: in fact, it is our own desires. Desires per se are not wrong. But they must be directed properly."

The room resounded with applause. Dust looked over the crowd with an obvious mixture of pleasure and indifference. He clearly relished this captive audience of attentive seekers, who worshiped him and hung on his every word.

The lecture closed on a note of sorrow, sorrow for our failures and frustrations. A general discussion followed, marked by outbursts of what seemed to be hysterical guilt. Each Family member in turn admitted his or her weaknesses, the sins and personal failures of his life.

Jacob surprised me by confessing.

"As a Jew, I realize that I must take personal responsibility for the death of Jesus. I crucified the Messiah and I continue to crucify him every day when I turn away from Heavenly Father."

I was amazed by his openness, and for the first time I felt compelled to share my own emotions with the group, although my main interest remained trying to understand the logic behind the lectures. When my turn to confess arrived, I spoke of the many times in my life when I had failed to live up to ideal standards, most recently the way I had shut out my parents whenever I came home from college for visits.

I was surprised at the comfort this confession gave me, almost a purifying feeling. Jacob exhorted us to "open your hearts" to Heavenly Father, explaining that this was our first chance to have a real relationship with God, and that God could enter our lives if we only repented sincerely. Those who were not sure about God should "try Him out," should direct their confessions to Heavenly Father.

Maybe they *do* have a relationship to God here, I thought. Maybe I was just not trying hard enough. Perhaps I should be less critical and more accepting. When I suggested this aloud, Jackie and Mitch broke into giant grins. I beamed back, warmed by their approval. Suddenly I understood what they wanted from me. Their role was to tease me with their love, dishing it out and withdrawing it as they saw fit. My role was not to question but to be their child, dependent on them for affection. The kiddie games, the raucous singing, the silly laughter, were all part of a scenario geared to help me assume my new identity.

Jacob took me by the hand and led me back to the lecture hall. Just play the game and see what happens, I thought. Give all of your effort to singing and dancing, to laughing and playing. Forget the critical Yalie for once. Join in the fun and, if you can't understand the lectures, try at least to remember them.

More singing and dancing preceded the next lecture. Family members swayed with their arms around each other, smiling and giggling. The heavenly kids began applauding madly, screaming and shouting when Dust announced he would now deliver his lecture on despair, clearly a Family favorite. He proceeded to talk about the failure of man to live up to his ideals and the calamity this incurred. My eyes watered as he launched into the problems of war, pollution, overpopulation, and starvation in frightening detail. Quoting Jesus and Confucius, he explained how we had failed God and the world:

"Half of the marriages in California are broken by divorce. Ten-year-old junkies roam the streets of Harlem. Our youth are aimlessly wandering, searching for lasting values. But all of our attempts in the past have failed. We can only look to God for hope. But God will leave His people if they fail Him...

Tears were streaming down the cheeks of the heavenly kids. Their faces reflected utter hopelessness and despair.

"Only a miracle can save this world," I heard someone whisper.

When the draining lecture finally ended, we sang a succession of mournful songs. Jacob was sobbing uncontrollably as he led us back into our discussion group. He started the conversation by telling how all of his attempts to live and work righteously had failed because "we just can't do it alone." Janis, a fellow group member, then spoke about the lack of food in the Third World countries, the fighting in the Middle East, the high unemployment rate in this country.

"Jacob's right. We can't do it on our own," she insisted. "Before I joined the Family, I thought that there was no hope for the world."

It was my turn to contribute:

"The lecture really depressed me. I admit there's a real chance of war between the Soviet Union and China and I don't see how we can right the imbalance between food production and overpopulation. It does seem as if maybe only God can help us resolve these problems. Maybe Dr. Dust has a point."

The words were out before I knew it.

Jacob beamed.

"That's real heavenly thinking, Chris. C'mon. I'll walk you to lunch."

Lunch was followed by dodge ball. This time I found myself playing much more actively. Instead of standing in the middle of the court, I watched the ball and moved accordingly. Jacob passed, patted me on the rump, and encouraged me to chant.

"Bomb with love. Bomb with love. Bombwithlove, Bombwithlove, Bombwithlove...." A gangly opponent fired the ball, hitting me in the nose. I moaned, covered my face, and walked off the court. Jacob hurried over and put his arm around me.

"Okay, now you just stand on the sidelines and chant as loud as possible," he said firmly. "Remember, the team that wins is the one that is most unified! Unity means everything in the Family, Chris. Now stop sulking and stand over here so you can chant for us."

I wiped the blood off my nose and softly chanted.

"Whatsamatter, Chris? We can't hear you. Chant louder," Jackie shouted. I complied.

"C'mon, you can chant louder than that." I chanted still louder. It suddenly flashed through my mind that I was beginning to automatically comply with any order I was given, but the thought was gone before it had really registered. The game soon ended, and we filed back to the Chicken Palace for our last lecture of the day.

If Dust's underlying motif in his previous talk had been despair, the theme of this one was hope.

"The union of consciousness, the technology and medicine of the space age, the growth of democracy, and the special privileged position of being in America at this time gives us the hope that if we are really unified, if we are really loving, if we find a group with sincere and effective religious guidelines, we can literally establish the Kingdom of Heaven on Earth.

"Consider, my friends, how what we do in this country is reflected and imitated throughout Europe and Asia. As goes America, so goes the world. And the Berkeley-San

Francisco Bay Area serves as the model for this nation. Every significant American social movement over the past fifteen years has begun here. America today is ripe and ready, awaiting the direction of the New Age. Our role here in Boonville, California, is to learn to serve each other and serve the world. If we can move the Bay Area, we can restore the entire country and serve the world according to God's plan." Dust's arms were outstretched toward the audience as if begging for acceptance of his offer.

Ecstatic applause! The heavenly kids got up as one onto their seats, shouting and clapping, whistling and cheering. Nancy picked up a guitar and started to lead the song:

> *We're His pride in the heavenly war, Unified Soldiers,*
> *Mightily, with one accord, we shall march, we shall march*
> *on....*

I softly joined in with the singing, Jacob holding my song-book and Jackie hugging me tight. The crowd began to sway together, arms on shoulders. Back and forth, back and forth in rhythm to the music. Jacob beamed at me lovingly.

"That's it, Chris, join in. It's all right. You've been found and you'll be saved with the rest of us." I tried to follow the words, but suddenly everything seemed to be moving too quickly. I felt faint, dizzy, sick inside. I just couldn't keep pace with the music. I turned desperately to Jacob, who was underlining the words in the songbook for me with his fingers. Much as part of me wanted to join in, my critical faculties rebelled. Something inside me was about to give, and I knew it.

Jacob looked at me as if to say: Are you ready yet? Can you abandon the so-called treasures you've worked so hard to earn, your academic prizes, your possessions, even your friends? Are you ready for us?

I began to sing louder and louder until I was putting in my 100 percent, "one-oh-oh!" as the Family called it. Ecstatically, I merged into the mass, tasting the glorious pleasure that accompanies the loss of the ego. How desperately I sought unity among people. How passionately I wanted direction, a clear path toward personal perfection. Could this be it—how could I know? But there was a chance, a precious, precious chance....

The crowd quickly dispersed for dinner, each group lining up on the lawn before the cooks in front of long tables. The servers ladled out a thick stew, a few pieces of beef strewn in among potatoes and carrots. We ate a happy meal interspersed with guitar music and folk singing. Each person was asked to sing a solo from the songbook. I chose "Getting to Know You" and Jacob sang "Climb Every Mountain." Jackie finished off with a rousing rendition of "The Impossible Dream." After dinner, Jacob passed out membership forms and firmly expressed his hope that I would stay on for a week.

I had been hearing all weekend about the wonderful series of week-long, in-depth lectures that would follow. Janis had insisted that I would find them brilliant, challenging, highly stimulating. True, I had not been impressed by the content of Dust's lectures so far, but I did feel a surge of warmth for the people here: their love, their hope, their dedication, their sincerity....As for my search for God—well, I just might learn something here. God just *might* be working through these people. What harm could it do to stay for a few more days?

I signed the membership form for the week-long lecture series as Jacob stood beaming at my side.

After breaking up the group, Jacob patted me on the back.

"Chris, I have a mission in the city. But you'll be hearing from me soon. I plan to send you a little gift. Until I see you again, keep listening and keep Heavenly Father on your mind."

He joined the other city-bound Family members who were now gathering up their things and heading for the parking area. After the buses pulled through the entrance gate to the Farm, slowly and ever so silently smiling young men replaced other smiling young men guarding the immense compound....

four/

When the buses had rolled out of sight, we circled up inside the Chicken Palace for a Sunday night songfest. Before the singing began, we introduced ourselves individually, beaming as we learned the names behind each face. Here was the warmth and free acceptance for which I had been searching. How different from college, where you could share a bathroom or classroom all year without really meeting, without truly bridging the gulf between two lonely people.

Joe, Susan, Bill, Jim, Janet, Andy—the names ran on and merged together as each of forty persons took his turn. Soon, we began singing, first a few Christian songs, starting with "Rock of Ages," and moving on through several others before reaching "Onward, Christian Soldiers." The singing worked its way up to a fevered pitch, with blaring of guitars and beating of drums. I noticed that the older members of the group sang with gusto, perhaps hoping to inspire newcomers to follow their example.

I stubbornly tried to hold back at first, to resist any attempt to make me sing louder or more forcefully than I wanted. I was suddenly aware of how my resentment had been building up all weekend, of how strongly I had resisted being coerced into participating in the group more than I desired. But all this was changing now. I was beginning to feel a genuine willingness to accede to the group's wishes, since there seemed to be some substance, some importance, to their movement. It was hard not to be impressed with the sincerity of each group member. It was difficult not to admire the atmosphere of harmony and control. I was fascinated by this living example of the dynamics of group membership, and I was determined to learn more.

Switching roles from lonely adolescent to amateur sociologist, I planned to explore the Family's ability to draw people together and generate such intense emotion. I realized by this time that I was in league with professional proselytizers, although I had no idea what it was they were up to or why. After all, I rationalized, if I found truths here worthy of attention, I could later share them with others. I need only consider the great religious movements of the past such as the congregations of America's Great Awakening revival—hadn't these people historically spent their lives attempting to forge human relationships founded on divine love? How many similarities did this mysterious Family have with other groups of its kin? What was its moving force, what was its guiding spirit?

Never for a moment did I underestimate the importance of my decision to continue with the group. But although I realized there was a certain risk involved, I never dreamed what the end result might be.

As I mouthed the words to the songs, I wondered how *I* would act if I felt I had stumbled on the secret of life as the Family seemed so sure it had. Wouldn't I fight to defend it? Wouldn't I live and die for it? Wouldn't I cautiously guard it, only revealing it to those who were fully prepared to accept it? Isn't all truth transmitted through mere mortals, subject to all the imperfections we call human? Shouldn't I then be tolerant of these enthusiastic, loving people around me who seemed to want so desperately for me to share their joy? Didn't I owe it to myself, as well as them, to spend the forthcoming week with them, sharing in their secrets, later to decide their worth for myself?

I looked down at my songbook to find I was verses behind. Quickly finding my place, I joined in at the top of my voice. . . .

While we sang on, a skinny little man slipped into the ramshackle Chicken Palace and proceeded to the front of the group, lecture notes in hand. After we sang one more verse, the guitarist put down her guitar. The little man stepped up promptly to the lectern.

"Hello, my name is Moses. Welcome to Boonville. I'm the advanced lecturer here and I'll be giving all the lectures for the coming week. If you have any questions, please save them until I've finished the lecture. Thank You."

Moses was an unimpressive, wimpy little fellow in his early thirties. Black frame glasses hung upon his knobby nose, behind which two dark brown eyes rested in sunken sockets. He had a pasty complexion, and as he spoke he displayed a distracting twitch in his left cheek. A limp jacket hung on his narrow torso, partially concealing a pair of corduroy pants which ended an inch or two above white socks. He wore beaten suede Hush Puppies which shuffled back and forth restlessly as he spoke.

I was astonished to see the effect this man had on the audience. As he began to speak, the Family members hurriedly closed their songbooks, settled down in their seats, folded their hands in their laps, and directed their gaze at him worshipfully.

"Tonight we are going to study God's plan for earth, the Principles of Creation," Moses began. He explained how God made each natural object to progress through three stages of evolution: formation, growth, and perfection. In perfection the object conforms to God's original intention. He compared this to the way a man builds a house. In formation stage the man has a blueprint and perhaps the foundation of the house. In the growth stage, the house is being built. In the perfection stage the house fulfills its original intended purpose.

What's he driving at, I thought. What's the intended purpose? I had hoped he would elaborate, but he lapsed into something about God creating everything with a polar nature. He explained that there are positive and negative elements in everything. He gave examples: an atom has an electron and proton, the earth and moon exist in polarity, male and female form positive and negative elements which attract each other in nature.

I scratched a few notes in a notebook I had been given at dinner. As I looked around I was struck by the concentration with which Jim, the Family member who had been assigned to be my host for the forthcoming week, was staring into Moses' eyes.

The little man continued, telling us that everything also has a dual character of inner and outer. Moses paused briefly to scribble "inner/outer" on a blackboard a freckled young lady had placed behind him and to scratch double arrows between the two words. He told us that God made man in His own image. He explained that man has male and female and inner and outer complements, for he has both a spiritual and physical nature. I guessed that he was presenting a pagan philosophy, but he started quoting from Genesis about man's relationship to God and God's plan for man.

Moses hitched up his pants as he spoke and he groped at the twitch in his cheek, as though by some sort of magic he could pull it off his face. Raising his voice, he continued:

"What did God want man to become?" He talked about something called "the four-position foundation" and something about a Universal Prime Energy.

Moses drew a diamond on the board with appropriate abbreviations, lines and arrows as he spoke. I squinted to make out the scribble, scratched my head, and tried to reflect on Moses' words. But before I could collect my thoughts, he was rattling on again, saying something about another type of energy called "Give and Take Action."

He quickly changed topics again, this time discussing Subjects and Objects with objects revolving around subjects like protons and electrons. God is intended to be the subject of all human relationships, he explained, and Man is to serve God as object. He then spoke about a natural division of subject and object in nature. Thus, in marriage, man is the subject and the wife is the object.

I wondered what the former feminists in the audience felt about these Master-Slave remarks which the Subject-Object jargon so strongly suggested.

As Moses droned on, I listened passively, occasionally jotting down notes. Family members around me were beginning to nod again. I was startled by the violence with which their neighbors rapped or shook them back to wakefulness.

Moses was now forty minutes into his lecture and moving at fever pitch. He concluded by telling us that God made us for the purpose of joy, joy in serving and joy in accepting service from others.

The audience roared with applause. Nancy snatched up her guitar and began a rapid song as Moses slipped out of the ramshackle hall. Everyone sang heartily, new converts using their songbooks and older Family members singing by heart. As I looked around the room, I was struck by the bizarre expressions on the audience's faces: they looked like eight-year-olds at a party, their salvation a birthday-cake panacea. How could people in their twenties and thirties have that look of blank innocence?

I seemed to be the only person not smiling, still puzzled, still attempting to understand the lecture. I knew that once I had looked through my notes I would have a whole rash of questions for this mysterious little man. The terms he used seemed obscure and indefinite. His subject-object jargon, for instance, confused and upset me. It was my understanding that all people were subjects in any relationship, that nobody could be reduced to the status of an object. I wanted to ask Moses about this important point. Didn't anybody *else* have questions? Why the immediate burst of singing? Why had Moses left without waiting for questions from the audience?

After the singing was over, I was quickly led to a newly formed group headed by Edie, a diminutive, apple-cheeked young woman with bright green eyes. She opened the session with a girlish smile which belied her brisk manner:

"All right, who has IN-spirations to share? Joe?"

Joe, a pockmarked youth, introduced himself as a devout Catholic and Eagle Scout from the Midwest who left his troop and his family three years ago to join the Family.

"I was so inspired by what a wonderful plan God has for us," he enthused. "Everything fits in so nicely with everything else. If only we could live heavenly lives with God, there'd be no crime, no poverty, only goodness and justice."

"Thank you, Joe. Any more inspirations?"

God, what stupidity, I thought. I had no inspirations, but I certainly did have questions:

"If God's plan for Creation is so great, why is there evil in the world?"

"Moses will explain that at the next lecture. Do you have any inspirations to share?" Edie seemed annoyed.

"Well, frankly, no. I am just trying to understand the lectures."

"Of *course* you are! Comprehension has to come from the mind before it comes through the heart. Keep on asking questions in our group, by all means. If I can't answer them, maybe somebody else can. All right, who else has an inspiration?"

Andy raised his hand.

"Listening to Chris, I became inspired that the Truth can appeal to different people in so many different ways. Chris is so intelligent and so well prepared to hear the Truth. Gee, I'm just so inspired by this whole group."

The group responded to Andy's enthusiasm with spontaneous patters of applause. I was struck by the way The Family clapped, like little children, hitting their first three fingers of the right hand against the left palm. When Edie whispered "Shhhhhhhh...," the patters quickly died down.

"Brothers and sisters," she announced, "tonight the wonderful cooks have prepared us a little treat. Let's all line up like good heavenly children for hot chocolate and brownies!"

Andy smacked his lips: "MMMmmmmmm....hot chocolate and brownies!"

We all filed off to a table in the back of the room. After snatching our goodies, we returned to our circle and sat cross-legged, beaming and munching away. Edie announced that tonight Joey, an older member of the Family, planned to "share" his Family story with us. We gathered around the smiling young man in gold-rimmed glasses perched on a stool, hands primly clasped in his lap:

"Tonight brothers and sisters," he began, "I thought I'd tell you about my introduction four years ago to the Family. Like many of you, I first met the Family when I was hitchhiking around the country. I'd finished my sophomore year at college, and frankly college had almost finished me. I was terribly disillusioned. I'd had a fight with my girl friend. My parents and I had been fighting on and off for several years. My life had no 'purpose and direction,' as we say in the Family. I wanted God's love. I needed God. I knew that He was somewhere and I must hunt Him down. So I quit school and hit the road. Ten days later I was in Berkeley where I met Rosie, one of the first people in the U.S.A. to become a Family member.

"After a week with Rosie and the Family, I realized how inadequate I was. Rosie, little pint-size that she is, took me over. She hollered at me just like my mother used to when I was a kid. In return for my obedience, she gave me direction. When it was time for me to find a job, she came along on every interview, straightening my tie, telling me not to slouch. She was my savior, my spiritual mother. I got into the habit of looking to her for help in every decision I made. Thanks to her love and guidance, I was able to get a respectable job and grow near to God in the Family. Our bonds were soooooo close. We shared *everything*!

"These are the types of relationships you find in the Family. You become really close to your brothers and sisters because you are so close to your Heavenly Father. I'll bet that after all of you have lived with our Family for a week, you'll want to stay for life! Thank you, brothers and sisters!"

Patters of applause, hundreds of fingers clapping against open palms. Brownies and sharing—a double treat for the evening.

Edie's group banded together once more. It was time to "cuddle," as Edie called it, wrapping each other in blankets and stretching our feet together in the middle of the circle. When we were all nice and cozy, Edie said, "Well, boys and girls, this is going to be a very special week for you. Let's share a prayer with Heavenly Father before we go to bed. Renee, why don't you pray for us?"

Renee, a pixie-faced young woman with freckles and a southern accent, intoned:

"Dearest Heavenly Father, oooooooooooothankYousoverymuch for this wonderful evening You have given us. Thank You for bringing all these children together to hear Your word, to experience the fresh air of the mountains, to spend a week together learning Your will for history. Be with each of this evening, Heavenly Father. Protect us from evil as we sleep, dear Father, and guide us in our groups this week. Aaaaaaaaaaa-men."

As we parted for the night, brothers and sisters briefly squeezed hands. Then the women set off for their trailer. When we had finished cleaning up the Chicken Palace and arranged our sleeping bags on the floor, I slipped out into the clear night for a moment, marveling at God's beautiful stars. Clear, clear, the air was crystal clear. Not a speck of pollution in the sky. This *must* be God's sky, God's earth, God's people, I thought. The people here were so incredibly nice to each other, warm, friendly—loving. I'd be damned if I was going to stop asking questions, but surely there must be something of value here!

I pulled my toothbrush out of my kit and headed toward the brothers' bathroom. Joe joined me in the bathroom, now filled with thirty group members patiently waiting in line. He told me how glad he was that I was staying for the week.

"You ask a lot of questions. You're really bright, Chris. I think you'll like it here a lot. If there's anything I can do to help you, just let me know." He hugged me and darted out the door.

How nice he was, how friendly and sincere. He didn't have to act or talk that way. Everybody here seemed to go out of their way for me, I reflected. I couldn't ask for a nicer group of people. Wouldn't it be great if all the things they were preaching were true....

As the line continued moving, I found myself in front of the sink. How curiously large it seemed. The bowl looked immense, much too big for my little hands. I suddenly thought of Alice in Wonderland and the magical potion that made her small. That was what a weekend with the group had done to me. Somehow the last two days had diminished me into a little child at summer camp, like all the others.

I glanced into the mirror as I brushed my teeth. Back and forth, up and down ... Suddenly, my hand froze. Foamy Crest toothpaste dribbled down my chin as I stared into the glass. I hardly recognized myself! My face was red and perfectly smooth. My eyes were wide as a child's, as round as oranges. My eyelids, which normally partially hooded my eyes, were now glued to the skin above them. The change frightened and fascinated me. I had the same glassy stare as all the others! I was one of them, then, wasn't I? I must be deeply spiritual after all, just like they'd said. Maybe that's why my eyes look so strange. But *why* glassy? Was this God's way of setting people apart, distinguishing His chosen people?

Amazed and slightly frightened, I headed back to the Chicken Palace to retire. Slipping off my jeans, I climbed into my bag and zipped it to my chin. I shook my head, wondering, wondering, wondering just what this magical world had in store for me. As I lay there drowsily, childhood dreams and fantasies mingled in my mind with images of chocolate-chip cookies and warm milk. I finally drifted off, carelessly running my fingers back and forth across the top of the bag, just as I used to do with my blanket as a child.

five/

"Where are you going, brother?"

"Out for a walk. Why?"

"New members aren't supposed to walk around here alone. I'd go with you, but I have two other guests to look after. Now, go back to sleep like a good brother. It's only six o'clock."

Offended at being ordered around like a child, I nevertheless did as he said, glumly returning to my sleeping bag and lying down in a row with fifty other brothers. Before dozing off, I asked myself: If these people can get me to give in so easily on little things, what can't they get me to do?

Twenty minutes later, Andy and Paul entered the hall, singing good-morning songs. As usual, older Family members popped out of their sleeping bags and stood at the sound of the first chord. Their instant attention amazed me. Jim and Jackie approached me from both sides and picked me up by the arms in unison. Before I knew it, I was on my feet like the others, into the bathroom and out in the five minutes allotted to me.

Out in the field, an older sister named Jeanie led the pack of overgrown youngsters.

"Gee, brothers and sisters! I have a great exercise for you to open up the week. We bend our knees way low to the ground, like this. Then we fold our arms into wings and waddle. Just like this, see?" And off she waddled around the circle, quacking away. All the men and women followed, giggling in procession.

"Hey, gee, that's great, just great, brothers and sisters. Now for another exercise." Jeanie sang: "You put your right foot in, you put your right foot out, you put your right foot in and you shake it all about.... Do the hokey-pokey and you turn it all around—that's what it's all about."

Tittering from the crowd as each person followed Jeanie's example to a T. The exercises continued with word games, imitating games, and other types of group participation. Anytime a new member slacked off, someone touched him or her on the shoulder and insisted:

"C'mon. You have to join in if you expect to have any fun."

After exercises, Moses announced the new groups for the week. My group was headed by Edie again. Other members included Jim, Keith, Scott, Chrissy, Doug, and Renee. I learned that Jim, Keith, Doug, and Renee had been members of the group for at least six months, while Scott, Chrissy, and I were still trying to orient ourselves in the group as newcomers. I sensed that all the guests shared my doubts and reservations about the Family.

Edie presided as our group gathered under a sprawling tree not far from the trailers.

"Good morning, brothers and sisters! This week we're going to grow so much closer together, closer than ever before. We have to think up a name for our group. How about the Honeybees? Renee?"

"How 'bout the Bugsinarug? We want to be as snuggly and close as three bugs in a rug."

"Any other suggestions? Okay Renee, we're the Bugsinarug. Why don't we sit tight in a circle and share? Who wants to share their goals for the week? Chris?"

"No, thanks, I'm not ready," I said cautiously. "Try somebody else."

Edie turned to Jim. I was curious to see what this veteran Family member would say. Jim responded: "Well, this week I want to have a giving heart. I want to experience Heavenly Father's heart, how He gives everything He has for His children. I want to be especially giving to Chris, who is my guest for the week. I want to show him life in the Family, how loving it can be."

"Keith?"

"I want to have a sacrificial heart, like Heavenly Father. I also want to pray at least three times today. I want to pray to hear the lectures with my heart. I also want to help Chrissy and Scott to understand our principles."

"Doug, what are your goals for the week?"

"I want to strengthen my relationship with Heavenly Father. I want all my relationships to be vertical as well as horizontal, centered on Heavenly Father's purpose. I want to listen to the lectures with all my heart and become a good object for Moses."

"Chris, what are your goals?"

I was ready now. "I want to understand all these principles you speak about, ask all the questions I need, and try to follow the examples of others in the group to test these principles."

"Thank you, Chris"—soft patters of fingers against palms—"you have your antennas up. I can tell you're going to become a great heavenly child."

"Renee, do you have some goals you would like to share?"

"Well, I want to become much closer to Heavenly Father's heart this week. I want to repent for my old life, to really ask Heavenly Father to forgive me and to show him I can be a good heavenly child. I also want to be a good object for Moses and for Edie. I want to have an inspiration to share after every lecture."

"Fine, Renee. Now, let's finish our breakfast quickly. I hear them singing in the Chicken Palace."

We set off for the lecture hall in a string, holding hands.

Needing to go to the bathroom, I dropped off the line. Immediately, Jim chased after me.

"What's the matter, Chris?"

"Nothing. I just want to go to the bathroom."

"You can't go now. The singing is starting. Go later. C'mon." He grabbed my arm and started towards the Chicken Palace. I complied resentfully.

The crowd was singing wildly by now, dancing up and down, jumping and clapping with abandon. The song was a wake-up for the sleepy guests. Jim and Edie positioned themselves on either side of me. Jim held the songbook and pointed to the words to be followed as Edie swung my hand back and forth to the music. Nancy was playing guitar up front again, breaking more strings in her fervor.

Kenny, whom Family members boasted about as a former rock star, was busy pound-pound-pounding to the children's songs, head bobbing back and forth.

The mood of the songs shifted suddenly and with it the older members seemed to grow sober on cue. As the group began to sing songs, traditional Christian hymns, they were transformed from a crowd of giggling youngsters to a somber, holy choir.

As I looked through the slats of the Chicken Palace walls, I noticed Moses descending from the hill, holding his notebook in his hands like stone tablets. The music ended as Moses walked in and took the platform. Clearing his throat, he spoke.

As he told us that the universe is "God's gift to man," he covered his heart with his hands to show how much Heavenly Father cared about us. I settled into my seat and noticed how Edie hung on every word that issued from the speaker's trembling mouth.

"The Creation is formed in time." He explained how all objects pass through the stages of perfection. Man lives in indirect dominion, needing to rely on God's message before he grows into direct dominion, when his will is one with God's. All the prophets served to convey God's message until men grew to perfection, according to Moses.

Moses jumped into an explanation of man's dual nature, that of spirit and flesh. God made the entire universe in two parts, the visible and invisible worlds. The invisible world is the world of spirit. Man has a physical or instinct mind and a physical body. But man also has a spirit mind and a spirit body—he has what Moses called an invisible "spirit man." The physical mind enables man to search for food and procreate the species, and the spirit mind is created to be the ultimate subject over the physical mind and body, for it is the source of the guiding virtues of love, truth, and beauty.

Moses paused for a moment, reamed his ear with a finger, then drew a stick figure at the intersection of two circles—presumably the physical and spiritual universes. His cheek began twitching again as he continued his lecture.

"All spiritual experiences are explained by the existence of the spirit world." He spoke about a world of "intellect, emotion, and will" which includes the spirits of all the dead people. He spoke of angels and other spiritual beings who exist in this visible world. If we only had our psychic senses open, we could see all this commotion clearly. Most of us, except for mediums and special prophets of God, remain blind to these events because we never fully developed. Why did we never fully develop? Moses told us that he'd cover that in the next lecture. "Now we'll pause to answer a few questions."

I raised my hand. Reflecting upon all the "spiritual" experiences people have spoken and written about for the past few years, I wanted to test his knowledge.

"How many dimensions are there to spirit world?"

"I really don't know. Next question, please."

Moses continued to answer questions about the lecture, but I sensed that he did not understand a good deal of what he had said. He seemed to accept most of the lecture on faith, for when someone asked a question, he would respond by mouthing slogans from his talk. His apparent ignorance annoyed me greatly, but I didn't challenge him further because of my own intellectual arrogance; I assumed, perhaps correctly, that most people didn't know very much about what they were talking about anyway, something I learned from college. As usual, I reasoned, I'd just have to pick and scratch for any answers myself. I had a dozen more questions to ask Moses, but why bother? He clearly had nothing to add.

After lecture and questions, we broke up into our small groups for lunch followed by a game of "Subject and Object"—a Family version of Follow the Leader which demonstrated the obedience one must have as an object to God and His disciples. New guests, the objects, imitated the gestures of their corresponding older Family members as they played subject. Edie, the head subject of the group, then called a halt and asked for more "sharing":

"Okay, brothers and sisters! Who's IN-SPIRED?" Edie cried.

Jim responded first:

"I was inspired by the greatness of these gifts. If we can only become perfect, what powers we would have to do good. When our spiritual senses are opened, how beautifully the world will radiate with the goodness of God."

Doug's turn in the circle was next:

"And when we perfect ourselves we'll no longer make mistakes, no longer perform evil acts. We'll live under the direct guidance of Heavenly Father. With no evil in the world, we can pursue righteous lives freely."

When Edie called on me, I replied:

"I still don't understand spirit world. What evidence do we have for the existence of this invisible world? I'm not so sure that all spiritual phenomena can be explained by the opening of one's senses. What evidence do we have for the three stages of growth? And I still don't understand how every relationship is one of domination."

"Just keep asking questions, Chris. The answers will come to you. If you have any real doubts or questions, just pray about them. Heavenly Father will answer your prayers, believe me. He always answers mine! This is a very special place and a special time, Chris, as you will learn as you live with us. Heavenly Father wants to tell you soooo much!!! Please be patient, Chris."

I glanced at Edie skeptically. Patience is fine, I thought to myself, but I wanted answers. Before I had a chance to record my question in my notebook, Edie took my hand and pulled me to my feet.

"It's time for some farm work. Okay, let's gather around front for assignments. It will do all of us a lot of good to work. Remember, heavenly kids, this is the opportunity for you to practice these principles. Chris, Chrissy, and Scott, I will talk to you all this afternoon about filling out some forms. We want to know *all* about you!"

Davey read the work assignments for each group. I was assigned to the trail crew, a group that was clearing a path up to the hills so that Family members could conduct spiritual hikes at sunset. After being given our picks and axes in the barn we proceeded to the trail. As we started to work, Edie shouted:

"Now, remember, first-weekers can't talk to first-weekers. Second-weekers can't talk to second-weekers. Promise you'll obey that!"

I resented this kind of regimentation, but I kept my mouth shut. The others individually replied with their okays. I looked down at the pick in my hand. My lily-white fingers looked so queer holding this earth-caked tool. I had done so little with my hands over the past four years except write within my ivory tower while my father toiled for the cost of my education. All my callous was on my thumb and index finger.

Seeing how awkwardly I was handling my pick, Scott stepped over to show me how to use it. As we worked side by side, he told me something about himself: that he was twenty-two, the son of a nuclear physicist, that he had intensively studied the Bible over the past few years, searching for answers about life. As we were chatting, Jim suddenly appeared at our side.

"Hey, you're both first-weekers! You aren't allowed to

talk to each other. If you want to know something or need help, just ask an older brother or sister. That's what we're here for. We've all been first-weekers. We know it's tough."

Annoyed at the interruption, I muttered "Okay," and picked away silently. Apparently sensing my anger, Jim suggested:

"How 'bout a song?" Did he really think he could dissipate my negative feelings that easily?

Jim distributed songbooks to the "new members," as first-weekers were called. All afternoon, we took turns singing religious and patriotic solos as everybody else busily picked and shoveled away. The hours passed quickly. My initial resentment toward Jim gradually melted away in the mass effect. About ten minutes before the work ended, Edie appeared and beckoned me to her side, smiling benevolently.

"How's everything going, Chris?"

"Fine. I still have a lot of questions, though."

She took my hand and looked me straight in the eyes. As her wide eyes gazed into mine, I felt myself rapidly losing control, being drawn to her by a strange and frightening force. I had never felt such mysterious power radiate from a human being before....

"Just wait, Chris," she said as she tightened her grip. "I'm certain that Heavenly Father will answer all of your questions for you. Heavenly Father knows you and we all love you. You are in good hands now, believe me. I'll try to answer all your questions and Moses will answer any questions I can't answer. And I want you to try to pray. Pray for answers. I pray for everything. Heavenly Father will answer you. He answers me. Sincerely try to listen, try to understand. You know that this is a special place. That's why we refer to the Farm as the Heavenly Kingdom. God is searching the world to call His children home, one by one. He loves you very much to go to the trouble of bringing you here. Try praying Chris. Just try it as an experiment." She sounded sensible. But I sensed that her appeal was much more subtle, touching something within me that undermined thought itself.

"Okay, Edie, I'll try. But I don't want to stop question-ing. I'm not satisfied with the answers I'm getting here. I've some serious doubts about the group."

"Everybody's suspicious at first. That will all pass with time. Chris, I'll pray especially for you. You're in the best of hands now."

After Edie had walked away, I approached John, the leader of the work crew. Clearing my throat, I asked the tall, sandy-haired young man in dirty coveralls, "Is it okay if I stop work for a few minutes? I'd like to try and pray."

"Pray? Of course. Take your time, Chris."

I hurried down the trail, climbed onto the rocks, and approached a nearby stream. The sun was piercing through the clouds, illuminating my way. I crossed the stream, sat down on a large boulder, and gazed up to the sky. After a few moments, I knelt and bowed my head in prayer:

"Dear God, Creator of this universe, I seek to know Your will. I seek to act righteously in Your world, to obey and serve my brothers and sisters. Please answer my questions, Heavenly Father. Please inform me about this mysterious place where I find myself. I love You and await Your response. Amen." It sounded somewhat like a business letter, this awkward prayer to God, that strange and unknowable being.

I looked upward again, my face illuminated by patches of sunshine bursting through the trees. I felt a lightness, a sudden coolness, as I stepped back across the rocks, listening to young voices floating toward me, united in happy song. God, dear God, if only You were true...

six

I awoke Tuesday morning to the sound of pounding rain. Exhausted by yesterday's nineteen-hour day, I slogged through the storm to the bathrooms.

After morning exercises, we met in our individual groups. Because of the weather, Edie's group gathered in the girls' sleeping quarters. It was the first time I had entered the trailer, which also contained the kitchen and Moses' private room. Edie got up from a corner of the tiny living room and hugged me as I entered. I beamed at her, happy to receive her mother love. As we settled down to breakfast, she gave us our instructions.

"Now, brothers and sisters, today's lecture is the most important of all. Moses will reveal to us why man has fallen from God, what happened in history to separate us from God. I want you to pay close attention to this lecture, especially you new members. Take careful notes and listen carefully to every word Moses says. Your very life depends on it. Now, who has goals for the day?"

I noticed that Renee was busily writing something on her hand. I had seen other Family members do this as a way of remembering their goals. As she began to speak, tears rolled down her cheeks.

"I want to be especially repentful today. I want to hear the words with my heart and ask Heavenly Father to forgive me for my awful sins. I want to pray three times today and be humble to my subject."

Jim spoke next.

"I want to be especially repentful for my crimes against God. I want to smash out Satan in my heart and be a guardian against Satan's attacks on anyone in the group."

This was the first time anyone in the group had mentioned Satan's name.

After several others had talked briefly, Edie concluded the group meeting by stating her own goals:

"I must repent sincerely to Heavenly Father today. I must recognize my guilt, that I followed Satan instead of God, that I commited the crimes of history, that I am totally responsible for evil in the world." I was astonished to see Edie break down and cry; Renee sobbed with her, head on Edie's shoulder, and Jim's eyes filled with tears.

We slowly started toward the Chicken Palace through the rain. Soft holy music and sweet chanting voices floated out of the lecture hall, enticing us as we entered. "Glory to Heaven and peace on Earth, Glory to Heaven and peace on Earth ... "over and over. The music was slow, high-pitched, and fervent, like an angelic choir.

Moses entered and sat down in the front row. He bowed his head in prayer as the music continued. As he raised his head, all Family members glued their eyes to his, gazing at him transfixed. Tears streamed down the women's somber faces. Moses rose after a few moments, and the music ended on the final verse.

"Okay, everyone, sit down quietly," he ordered, and the audience dropped to their seats en masse.

Outside, the storm continued to rage. Occasional bursts of thunder dramatized the atmosphere in the Chicken Palace.

The Family

Rain splashed and pattered on the tin roof, breaking the oppressive silence. As Moses rose, a number of people in the audience bowed their heads in prayer, sobbing quietly as the rain dribbled off the roof into small pools and rivers.

Moses spoke sternly, with the authority of a prophet:

"Today we are going to talk about the Fall of Man! We will tell why man never achieved perfection, why evil exists in the world, why we are separated from our lonely Heavenly Father."

Moses instructed us that the answer lies in Genesis. But Genesis is merely a book of code, according to him. Up until this moment, God could never speak directly to man. Man could never understand this code. But through deep prayer and hard, sacrificial work, we are finally able to break the code and comprehend the symbols. The wispy little man turned and scratched a few lines on the blackboard with his chalk stub.

"For the root of sin let us turn back to the Bible." In Genesis, he explained, we have two symbols called the Tree of Life and the Tree of the Knowledge of Good and Evil. The Tree of Life stands for the perfection of Adam; if Adam had grown to perfection he would have had immortal life in spirit world and continuous enjoyment of the physical world.

The other tree in the Garden, the Tree of the Knowledge of Good and Evil, stands for Adam's object, Eve. Moses never explained why, so this didn't make much sense to me. But I did my best to follow as he continued.

As he spoke, Moses pointed to the chalk lines, adding a few letters that I assumed were the names of the primordial couple. He was beginning to work himself into a frenzy, gesticulating with his soft, white hands as he spoke. The audience sat spellbound. Those who weren't crying or praying stared directly into Moses' glassy brown eyes, as if searching for the light of God.

"In the book of Genesis we ask ourselves, What is the identity of the serpent?" The serpent is Satan, the archangel, according to Moses. He explained that Satan was intended to be the servant of man, an intermediary between man and

God. In these early times, before man was created, Satan was treated by God as a true son, and Satan grew to love God very much. Moses revealed to his bewildered audience that God gave Satan all the knowledge of the universe and all types of power in spirit world so that he could guide men. Next, God created Adam, whom He loved very much. He loved him so much that He gave 70 percent of His love to Adam and only 30 percent to Satan. Now, Satan grew jealous of Adam. He wanted all of God's love, not just as a servant but as a son. Moses went on and on with the details of these divine secrets.

"After Adam, God created Eve in body and spirit." God also loved Eve as a daughter, the little prophet explained. Eve and Adam grew through formation and growth stages with the guidance of God's words and the commandments not to touch the fruit of the Tree of Knowledge of Good and Evil. In other words, God told man to resist temptation, the temptation of love and wisdom without God's blessing.

"Now, Satan loved Eve very much." He spent a great deal of time with Eve and enjoyed the love Eve gave him. Moses raised his voice as he rapidly related how Eve often left Adam's side to play with Satan all day, going for long walks with him. This was carelessness on the part of Adam, for Eve was never supposed to leave his side, according to Moses. Satan loved sharing secrets with Eve. Eve grew fond of Satan's wisdom and decided to spend more and more time with him.

Moses leaned over and circled two of the stick figures vigorously. A look of intense anger flashed across his face as he continued.

He told us that the spiritual Fall of Man started one day when Satan seduced Eve, having sexual intercourse with the spirit body of Eve. Eve, who grew to love this very much, went back to Adam and tempted him with her new-found love. Moses revealed that this is the hidden meaning of the apple in Genesis, for the apple represents Eve's sexual love. Eve seduced Adam, who fell both spiritually and physically since both spirit and physical bodies were involved. Man failed God, breaking His commandment. He took the fruit of the Tree of Knowledge of Good and Evil. Realizing what he had done, man was ashamed, Moses said as he shook his head. He and Eve then covered their lower parts, as it is written in Genesis. When God visited them in the Garden one day, He saw Adam and realized that he had committed sin. "How sad was our Heavenly Father," Moses cried. After the painstaking effort of God to create a perfect universe for man, man had failed God. "How Heavenly Father cried!"

The rain smashed violently upon the tin roof. The sky was alive with lightning. Great bursts of thunder exploded through the pounding downpour. The heavens seemed to cry out, asking to be heard. Moses suddenly burst into tears.

"Oh, how Heavenly Father cried! How many days—days and nights He cried! He cried for you, and you, and you, and you!" Moses stabbed at the audience with his bony finger.

"The whole of human history is the attempt of man to come back to God." When man fell, the universe fell. Ever since that day, man has been filled with self-centered love, following his evil ways as Satan grows in power.

By now the audience was consumed with loud wailing. Many of the women were sobbing hysterically. A woman near me screamed, "I'm sorry, Father!" Jim quickly took her hand and began to comfort her. Yet, in spite of the super-charged atmosphere, I noticed that some group members were fighting to stay awake....

The rain smashed down more violently than ever. Several Family members around me began whispering nervously as the room's lights flashed on and off.

Somebody hissed: "It's Satan! It's his demons! They're controlling the electricity. They're trying to stop the lecture!" A woman near me nodded with a shudder. Chills crawled up my spine as lightning bolts crackled outside. Moses continued.

"What is the result of the Fall of Man? Satan, now completely fallen from God, seeks the love of all men." He will therefore tempt us constantly, trying to win our love and affection, Moses warned. Man is condemned to mortality. He is condemned to working the cursed soil for food. His wife will be completely obedient toward him and will feel an urge toward him. Only in the Family, only in the Family, he repeated, can we come back to God. Only here can we learn to defeat Satan and establish an eternal relationship with Heavenly Father which will save us from being crushed by Satan.

"I want you to rise and sing 'Holy, Holy, Holy.' As you sing, you must think of our dearest Heavenly Father, how we failed our dearest Heavenly Father, who longs, who longs so much for us." Moses bowed his head.

The women blew their noses and wiped away their tears as we sang, very slowly, with great emotion. "Holy, Holy, Holy" was followed by a simple Family hymn with vague references to "Father" and "Our Master." Then, ever so reverently, we filed out in funereal procession as Moses headed off toward his private room.

Edie's group reconvened behind the Chicken Palace after the rain had ended. Edie and Renee were sobbing again. Finally, Edie pulled herself together and asked for inspirations. Jim began:

"I'm inspired by how beautiful a life we can have if we can only come back to God. Only in the Family have I ever seen people who really repent for Adam's sin and try to return love to God. Family life makes it so much easier to repent and become perfect."

Now it was Renee's turn: "I'm so sorry that I have failed to listen to God. I'm so sorry that I as Eve fell with Satan and tempted Adam. All sisters must feel this way. It was I, I who fell. It was *I* who interfered with God's perfect plan. Forgive me, Heavenly Father, forgive me, brothers and sisters, for my sinful past!"

Renee rubbed her freckled face and bowed her head in shame.

After calling on Keith and Doug, Edie turned to me for a response.

"If what Moses says is all true, then man committed one

simple crime and thus fell away from God. The restoration of man back to God must be fairly easy."

"You're so smart, Chris," Edie replied. "Just wait until the next lecture. I want to stress the positive aspect of this lecture. We all share original sin because of our fall from God. But in the Family we can restore ourselves, restore the universe, by leading repentful lives and living by God's commands. God has given us many simple truths to follow in the Principle. All we must do is listen to God, obey the Principle, and become good objects for His love. The next lecture will cover the path of salvation, which we can attain only in this beautiful Family of ours."

Chrissy and Scott seemed to share my reservations about the lecture. They voiced their doubts after lunch. Chrissy spoke first:

"You know, it doesn't make sense that all of man's crime and sin stems from one sexual act. And that business about the spirit world is ridiculous! How could Eve have sex with an angel? I just don't see how man's fall can begin with one simple act."

"I can't accept that either, Edie," Scott added. "How can man fall from one act to murder, steal, and cheat his brothers and sisters? What kind of plan would God have for the universe if it could be destroyed so easily? And doesn't that make God seem less than all-powerful?"

"Truth is truth, Scott," Edie insisted. "I can't explain it further except to say that the Bible records it. It's there for your inspection. God's universe is very fragile. And man's faith in God is equally fragile. If you violate that faith, it's very hard to purify yourself and come back to God. On the other hand, the more evil you do, the easier it is to be evil. You're very bright, Scott. You'll catch on, I'm sure.

"Well, brothers and sisters," Edie concluded brightly, "It's time to gather for work. The rain has stopped, so we can all work on the vegetables or the trail."

Refreshed from our sharing, we were eager to get to work. Edie had one last commandment:

"Remember, brothers and sisters! This is your chance to

Ac-tualize the Principle, to really put it into practice. Work prayerfully and repentfully and Heavenly Father can help you."

We sang as we worked on the trail. Everything was so peaceful after the rains. Birds flew through the treetops, the sun warmed us gently. Who could help but marvel at the wonder of God's earth, God's sky?

Yet the God they spoke of here, this Heavenly Father to whom they prayed, was so strangely unfamiliar to me. My God was a pantheistic one, springing from rocks and trees. This new God was a guiding father burdened with irresponsible sons and daughters. How much I wanted to believe in their God! What a comfort to know that he had predestined his children to hear the Principle, that we were a special elect which had been preparing all our lives for this moment. Although the lectures had yet to mention it, Edie had made it clear that we each had special missions, special reasons for being here at this time. Looking back on my college years, I could see how there might be a pattern that had led me to this place.

I wanted so much to be able to pray to a God Who actually listens. I wanted so much to have a relationship with my Creator, yet I had never been able to do this. I had been afraid to pray, afraid of the immensity of the forces with which I would have to contend, afraid of how small I must stand in comparison with God. I suddenly remembered sitting in the redwood forests of California and how I had wondered about the history of those giants. Their age and size overwhelmed me, making me feel so small. Think of the stories they could tell! I must hurry and come to grips with my own mortality, for I would perish long before those steadfast giants, those massive monuments to a seeming eternity.

I started working on the trail, picking away at the unyielding soil. As I hacked away, I began singing along at the top of my voice with my brothers and sisters. After all, the only way for me to surely know if this was my destiny was to try it out, to really participate. I swung and swung my pick, lacerating the tender skin on my fingers. My right hand began to blister, then the blisters broke. I continued to pick and dig until I noticed blood oozing from one of my wounds. I showed my hand to my work leader, who told me to go back to the kitchen and wash it.

After cleaning and bandaging my hand, I met Edie on the way back to the trail:

"Chris, I've been praying a whole lot for you. And I want you to know that Heavenly Father wants you here so very much. He loves you and misses you, has missed you for six thousand years, ever since we fell from God. I wish we had more brothers and sisters like you. I feel very close to you."

I smiled.

"Well, I feel very close to you, Edie."

"That's as it should be, Chris," she said calmly. "After all, I *am* part of your spiritual lineage, related to your spiritual father, Jacob. Many good spirits work through our Family at Boonville. But there are many evil spirits here as well. Have you noticed the way people in lecture tend to fall asleep? Well, that's due to the sleepy spirits. They press on your eyelids and close your eyes. Davey, the Farm's crew leader whose spiritual senses are open, has actually *seen* them during lectures. They sit on your shoulders and wait for an important segment of the lectures. Then they press on your eyelids and close your eyes. We knock 'em off each other with our knuckles. And you know why we pop out of our sleeping bags each morning—'jump it,' as we say in the Family? That's to shake off all the sleepy spirits who cling to our bodies when we're sleeping. Now, I'm not really supposed to tell you this before the lecture covers it, Chris, but I think you are especially perceptive. Please don't repeat it to any of the other first-weekers! Do you have any questions?"

All I *had* were questions. My search for self-understanding had brought me three thousand miles to this mysterious paradise. How could I swallow such "Heavenly Secrets," as they called them? I knew that the Bible referred to angels and spirits of all sorts, and I had read many tales of mediums in trance who had seen such wonders. Since I could not check these things out for myself, what could I do but trust? And the people in the Family did appear so sincere, so trustworthy... How or why could such loving, innocent people even dare to fabricate such stories, especially when they were so aware of God's love and judgment?

I worked harder than ever all that afternoon, hacking at the stubborn California soil. As I labored, my hand became a bloody mess under my bandage. If what the Family was telling me was true, I told myself, then I must participate fully every moment. I had a long history of sin, and Edie had said that working in the Family showed God how sorry you were for your wrongdoings. People told me that, through diligent effort, I could attain my salvation as well as the salvation of my ancestors in spirit world.

On and on I worked. Everyone around me seemed to be working just as hard or harder, frantically digging and picking at the soil. I finally could pick no longer. My bandage was soaked with blood and my arms were like lead. I started to cry like an exhausted child, wiping away the tears with the large, ragged sleeve of my old farmer shirt. Finally, I asked Jim if I could stop for a while and pray. He nodded.

I crossed the riverbed, returning again to my private spot. Sitting down on the boulder, I closed my eyes and bowed my head.

"Dear Heavenly Father, I don't know if this is the place where You want me to be. So much of what they say sounds true. So much of it I want to believe. Please tell me if this is my mission. Tell me if this is my destination. Tell me what I must sacrifice in this most difficult journey. A-men."

Sobbing, I returned to the group, only to find that work was over for the day. It was dinnertime: zucchini, tomatoes, and beans laced with cheese. Everything was fresh, picked from our own fields, and, after a day out of doors, I was starving. We ate in large circles, Moses sitting in front of a huge, crackling fire which sent great orange sparks flying into the cold, black sky. I watched the way various older Family members vied to sit as close to their great prophet as possible, imagining perhaps that some of God's love energy would be transmitted to them from their leader.

Different work groups entertained as we ate, singing songs whose verses they had composed while working. The same themes ran through all of them, telling how desperate the singers had been before joining the Family and how wonderful Family life could be. Every song was dedicated to Heavenly Father first. The verses stressed Heavenly Father's love, how Heavenly Father was building His Heavenly Kingdom in Boonville. Overwhelmed by the day's testimonies and inspirations, warmed by this Family atmosphere, I beamed at my newfound brothers and sisters, their loving faces lit by the dancing flames. The happy evening ended with a prayer by Moses under the stars:

"Dearest Heavenly Father, we wish to thank You for bringing us together this day to hear the Principle. Help us to hear each word with our hearts as well as our minds. Protect us from evil spirits as we sleep, and guide us in our individual missions. We pray this humbly and sincerely in our Master's name. A-men."

Our Master's name? Did he mean Jesus? But this was not exactly a Christian theology they were teaching here.

After the group broke up, I walked over to the girls' trailer. Entering, I headed for Moses' door. It bore a makeshift cardboard sign decorated with flying angels. The sign read:

PRAYER ROOM. PLEASE DO NOT DISTURB

I knocked softly and Moses soon appeared.

"Come in, Chris," he said quietly. "How are things going?" Putting his hand on my shoulder, he drew me into his modest quarters and beckoned me to sit down.

"Fine, just fine, Moses. But I still have a great many questions, and I thought I'd come directly to you. I just don't understand all this business about a spirit world. How can we know directly about a world that we are participating in but of which we are not fully aware? I mean, you can't even *see* this so-called spirit world."

"You can only know all this through deep prayer and faith, Chris. Just follow the Principle in your daily practice, and the knowledge will come to you. There are many forms of knowledge of the spirit world which older Family members have experienced. They will tell you when you have been prepared. Remember, this is just your first training session. As the weeks go by, you will assimilate this special knowledge very quickly."

"Tell me something, Moses," I insisted. "Who founded these principles? And who went to all the trouble to assemble these truths?"

"Reverend Moon. Sun Myung Moon is our teacher. We follow everything he says, for he is a prophet sent by God."

Moses smiled, and I responded with a quizzical look. I remembered reading in *Newsweek* eight years before about a Korean evangelist named Moon who married hundreds of couples at once. His following, I recalled, claimed he was the Messiah. But even at the age of thirteen I had learned not to take what I read in magazines too seriously.

I continued to question Moses.

"How did this Reverend Moon arrive at these principles?"

"Through prayer and battle deep in spirit world. Before he was told by God of Satan's crime, he had to wrestle with Satan himself, as Jacob had to wrestle the angel in the Bible. It took nine long years of tearful prayer. He had to pray for each question individually. He had to go to each great teacher to learn his spiritual secrets. He went to Moses, Buddha, Jesus, Confucius. He had to serve each master until the master revealed his secrets. When he finally was certain of all these principles, he asked God Himself. Heavenly Father, as a test of Reverend Moon's faith and certainty, replied no the first two times he asked. On the third try, He finally admitted that Reverend Moon was right. On that day, everybody in spirit world bowed to our Master. It was a glorious day for mankind, for Reverend Moon was now capable of fulfilling the mission Jesus never completed."

"But how can I accept all this, Moses? How am I supposed to believe you?"

"The question is, Whom do you trust? As Jesus said, you shall know the vine by its branches, you shall know the tree by its fruits. If you ever begin to doubt these principles, just look at the splendid examples your brothers and sisters are making for you. Look at their virtue, their righteousness. You will then be convinced that they are living by the Truth."

"Thanks, Moses. I guess I'll just have to think about it."

"Thank you for coming. And welcome to our Family," he softly replied.

My head swimming, I returned to the Chicken Palace to sleep. Jim and Jackie were waiting up for me. Didn't they trust me to get to bed on time? I spread out my bag between them, slipped inside, and glanced over at my companions. Through the moonlight I saw Jim and Jackie immediately assume the mantis position for evening prayer. Jackie's face was red with emotion. Sweat dripped from his brow, and tears streamed down his cheeks. Resting on his elbows, he clenched his hands together. They shook fitfully as Jackie mumbled his prayer. "Smash out Satan, smash out Satan, smash out Satan!" were the only words I could hear. He swung his right hand around and punched viciously at the air. His forehead was ringed with sweat, beads dropping off onto his bag. Jim, praying on my left, mumbled, "Thank You, Heavenly Father, thank You, Father." His cherub's face, with its rounded features and almond eyes, looked so peaceful. Yet, like Jackie, he was crying as he prayed. From time to time Jim started to fall asleep. Every time his head dropped, he awakened again to offer more pleas. His prayer followed this cycle for fifteen or twenty minutes. Finally, he dropped his head and settled into sleep in a crouched position.

Closing my eyes, I uttered a short prayer, echoing the prayers of the day:

"Dear Heavenly Father, please guide us daily. We thank You for this wonderful Creation and hope we can live up to Your plan for us. Guard us against the Evil One, and keep us safe this evening. We ask you *in the Master's name*. Thank You and a-men."

I drifted off to sleep after my cathartic prayer. Later that night, I awoke with a start to the sound of marching feet.

Looking up, I saw several older Family members filing past me. Freshly showered and dressed in dark suits, their hair slicked back and gleaming in the moonlight, they stepped together as one. The very rhythm of their steps frightened me, for they moved like marching dolls, like soldiers or androids, marching back and forth, filing out the door into the darkness. Each movement was perfectly choreographed. Just like the lectures, like the games, I thought, with no time to reflect, no opportunity to think. Everything moved in exact procession, minds being turned and twisted one by one. Fully awake now, I suddenly realized how frightening my situation was. They were attempting to control me here, to turn me into one of *them!* I wanted to scream, but screaming would only send one of those wooden dolls after me. All right, Chris, let's get out of this place!

I'd try to escape at dawn. I simply couldn't take the chance of running through the fields and climbing the fence in the dark tonight. I might get caught on the barbed-wire fence, which could be electrified, and then I'd be done for. If they caught me trying to escape, there's no telling what they'd do to me. No, I'd wait till sunrise and make a break for it then. I had to move quickly while this moment of insight lasted, before they were able to work my mind over again, making me completely theirs. If I stayed, they'd surely eventually get the obedience and compliance they wanted, turning me into a robot like the others. How could I have been such a fool not to realize this before? Gotta get out. Got to. All right, at dawn then. I'll do it at dawn. I have to escape, to escape for my very life.

seven / "*You are my sunshine*, my only sun-
shine ... jump it brothers! Everybody up."

I staggered to my feet, my heart pounding. In my
exhaustion I'd slept through my one chance to escape! Well,
I'd just have to wait it out until tomorrow morning. I'd
probably be watched all day by Jackie and Jim. But if they left
me alone for even a moment, I'd make a run for the gate.

I was suddenly aware of a throbbing pain in my hand.
Removing the grimy bandage, I saw that it was badly infected
and beginning to swell. I would have to get to a hospital as
soon as possible.

We gathered in the usual circle for exercises after wash-
up, then broke into our groups. Edie ordered Renee and me
to pick up the breakfast. As we headed toward the kitchen,
Renee confided:

"You know, Chris, I led a very bad life before I came to
the Family. That's why I cry so much. I did all sorts of nasty
things. But the principles say that Heavenly Father can

77

forgive me. He'll forgive you too, you sinful boy." She waggled her finger at me playfully and winked. As we walked back to the group with the breakfast, she added:

"I know Heavenly Father wants ya here with us. I feel he's tryin' extra hard to get through to you. You really oughtta pray to him about everything. Now, watch that you don't spill that milk on your pants, you silly boy!"

As we arrived, Edie was addressing the group:

"Okay, brothers and sisters, let's share again! I'm writing my goals on my hand so I don't forget them, so you do the same and learn to imitate your subject. Who has goals? Chris, you look so glum! Don't be sad! What goals do *you* have for today?"

I thought to myself: to get out of this crazy place! "I don't have any goals yet; call on me later."

"Okay, Jim, what goals do you have to share?"

"I want to be more sincere and giving today. I want to help all the guests, especially Chris, with their spiritual problems. I want to understand the Principle with all my heart. Also, I want to give something to someone today without taking credit for it."

The other members of the group shared in clockwise fashion. Fortunately, Edie didn't call on me again. She obviously sensed that something was wrong, so she called me over to her side.

"What's the matter, Chris?" Again her eyes probed mine, leaving me trembling. Was there no way to hide my escape plans from her?

"Edie, I'm thinking of leaving. I simply don't have the opportunity to think for a moment here. It's, it's just too much pressure. I've got to go off on my own and reflect for a few weeks before I can make any commitments."

"Chris, you can't! This is the most important time of your life. You have to promise me one thing." She grabbed my hands and clasped them firmly. "Promise me you'll stay to hear all the principles. Give yourself a chance to practice the Principle and learn about our life style. Promise me, Chris!"

Overwhelmed by the forces of fear and love within me, I found myself giving my word. Edie smiled and hugged me.

"Now, go inside like a good brother and listen to the lecture." I headed toward the shack with a sinking heart. How was she able to get me to agree with her?

Jim ran out of the Chicken Palace to greet me:

"Hey, yay, have a great day!" he shouted. "What's the matter, Chris? We don't allow long faces here. Everybody's got to be happy!" He led me inside by the hand.

The singing lasted for about fifteen minutes. Members joyfully swayed back and forth, arms atop shoulders. By the time the music stopped, I had forgotton my lapse into disbelief.

Moses rose and began the lecture session with a short prayer. After the prayer, he hitched up his pants and began what Edie had advertised as "The most inspiring lecture you'll ever hear."

"The title of this lecture is 'The Fulfillment of Human History.' The history of man is the history of man's efforts to come back to God." And so Moses launched into another lecture, but this time he spoke with cheerful exuberance. All through history God has been guiding and preparing man to return to God, to share in His love. With the Fall of Man, man failed to fulfill his purpose and the purpose of Creation. Moses promised us that man can work to come back to God, for God has prepared a universe where penance is possible through the principle of indemnity. By paying indemnity with hard work and suffering in this world, man can return to God. Moses assured us that through prayer, God can be convinced to give His grace to man, to actually shorten the amount of work man has to do to fulfill his purpose.

His voice ringing with conviction, Moses went on to explain how man has worked to receive grace from God through all sorts of prayer and intense suffering. When enough indemnity has been paid, God will allow mankind to come back to Him so the Kingdom of Heaven can be proclaimed on earth. The crucial times when man comes close to attaining this goal are called the Last Days.

Jesus' time was the Last Days, as were Noah's, Moses explained. Each time God has especially prepared the Israelites to set the foundations for the salvation of man. The Second Coming of Jesus will also mark the Last Days.

Moses dropped his voice, licked his lips and turned the pages of his large black notebook. I wondered where his lecture was leading us.

"What are the 'signs' of the Last Days?" he asked rhetorically. Moses quoted from selected biblical verses, all of which talked about the judgment of Heaven and Earth by fire and the resurrection from the dead. He also told how in the present age the three blessings of God are being restored.

"In the Last Days, the Bible predicts men shall rise from their tombs. This means the resurrection of spirit men." In the Last Days, good and evil spirits will have more and more influence on world events, he claimed. Spirit men can actually grow closer to God by hearing the Truth and working through the spirits of the people on earth. According to the lecture, if you hear the Truth, your ancestors will push you to Ac-tualize the truth.

"In these Last Days, Christian spirit men can grow out of Paradise, the growth stage of spirit world, and into Heaven, to be one with God. Many spiritual phenomena occur as spirit men anxiously try to influence events on earth."

In the Second Coming, all spirit men are allowed to hear the truth, Moses assured us. Just as Christian leaders will get the chance to hear the message, so all religious leaders will be given the chance to commit themselves to the Truth. Buddhist spirit men, for example, can work to bring Buddhists on earth to the Lord of the Second Coming.

"Predestination is another phenomenon of the Last Days. Heavenly Father can work to bring the best representatives to salvation first." Moses emphasized that if you have a specific mission, Heavenly Father may call you. If you are called, you are the most qualified person God has available. If you fail your mission, somebody else will be predested to take your place. Moses now quoted several short Bible verses concerning predestination. Then he rapidly closed the meeting with a prayer thanking God for the honor of delivering this lecture and asking that spirit men help usher in the Lord of the Second Advent.

Riotous singing followed, as usual. The message was one of hope, one of overcoming. Nancy played her five-string guitar frantically to further stir up the enthusiasm as eager Family members bobbed up and down, shouting to the music.

Following the songs, Edie opened up our group discussion with an inspiration:

"I'm just so glad that we know these are the Last Days. We should be very grateful that we have been handpicked by Heavenly Father to follow Him and fulfill our individual missions. I hope I can be worthy of this honor. Renee?"

Renee closed her eyes in prayer as she always did before she spoke, then after a moment's hesitation began:

"I am so inspired by the guidance that Heavenly Father has given us. He continues to keep us out of danger, to send us the best people he can find, to give us the food and clothes upon our backs."

Keith picked up the pace of the sharing: "Heavenly Father has given us a great chance to show our gratitude to our ancestors for bringing us here. Imagine this: An ancestral spirit man can grow to perfection, to become one with God, if he only works to guide and help those of us in the Family! What a wonderful service we can perform for them as we serve Heavenly Father!

"But we must be very careful to follow Heavenly Father. We are so far from God that we cannot know Him except through the Lord of the Second Advent. It is our duty to recognize him first."

"But who's the Lord of the Second Advent?" I asked.

Jim responded: "You'll know by the time the lectures are completed." He continued: "What I find most inspiring about the lecture is the way it explains all of human history. All history is the attempt for men to work through God's laws, to restore the universe and attain salvation. The beauty of this plan will be seen in the next few lectures."

That sounded reasonable enough. Could I have misinterpreted what I'd seen the night before? After all, if this was the Truth and I knew it to be so, I would do everything in my power to keep people here until they had heard everything, to train them to believe. But I still felt a great need to take a step back and look at the whole set of lectures in a way I could never do here. If I could only return to New Haven...

"Chris, Chris! You're dreaming. No more spacing out! C'mon, pay attention to us and follow center. I'm the center man here; that means God's speaking through me, so you listen up! How do you ever expect to grow in the Family otherwise? And your Heavenly Father needs you *so* badly!"

We broke for lunch, singing merrily before we ate. I had sung more here in the last five days than I had ever done in my life. Like most of the newcomers, my voice was hoarse and raspy.

At lunch Renee very carefully peeled and sectioned an orange, placed the sections in the form of a circle, and offered the fruit up to Edie, Heavenly Father's representative in the group through whom God spoke directly. She gave away the rest of her lunch as well, her cookies to me and her sandwich to Chrissy. I noticed that Jim did the same thing. It was as though one got brownie points for righteousness, each helpful act being a devoted gift to God. So this was what was known as paying indemnity. The whole process of restoration seemed to be founded on this concept—showing God that you cared so much that you were willing to sacrifice and suffer.

After lunch and sharing, we went to work. Fearing the swelling in my badly infected hand, I spoke to Edie about it. She replied that this was a good sign of God's work:

"Sure, you're paying indemnity. Your hand was injured because of all the sins you have committed against God. But if you work faithfully, God can use your injury to claim you away from Satan's world. Just pray for it and it will go away by God's healing."

As a physician's son, I was naturally wary of this form of medication. But I could no longer view the Family's practice with an outsider's dispassion. I had entered a new phase, a stage of experimentation, in which I felt impelled to behave as they instructed, at the same time trying to maintain my identity and powers of rational thought. I saw this participation not as a blind doing but as an experimental "let's try it their way" attitude. Yet I knew that my rationality was eroding under the relentless bombardment of lectures, "inspirations," and constant hand-holding, and the annoying grinning the group called "love bombing."

I asked Edie for permission to pray and walked over to my special place. The stream sang out, gurgling and bubbling delightfully. It seemed to be singing a song to me, a happy song of water slapping rock. Suddenly, the world seemed as though it were made expressly for me. Birds called out, cows lowed in the distance. All Creation was mine, a gift from God! Was this the Heavenly Father of whom they spoke? I wondered as I knelt in prayer:

"Dear God, or Heavenly Father, or whoever You are … If it is possible to take my swollen hand as a sacrifice done in Your service, then please accept it. Please help me to understand these lectures and come to know Your will. Amen."

The next three days flew by, one day blurring into the next. Moses gave new, highly systematic lectures on the providence of restoration, as reflected in the Bible. He began with restoration centered on Adam's family, telling how Cain and Abel were supposed to unite together with a common faith in God. Cain's killing of Abel gives rise to a whole series of historical problems of the Cain-Abel position and set the foundations of faith and substance. Everything must be restored on individual, family, tribe, nation, and worldwide levels; God originally intended Adam to be the faithful leader and father of mankind on all these levels. Noah's and Abraham's family accomplished on some but not all of these levels. Moses, after a period of faithlessness by his people, finally managed restoration by leading his faithful on the national level. This was preparation for restoration on the worldwide level, the coming of the Messiah.

Bombarded by theory, I struggled to stay awake, learning to smile on cue, wearily trying to reflect on the new and undefined terms Moses used.

According to the lectures, Jesus was sent to become the Second Adam. Indemnity had been paid through history on all other levels. It was the mission of the Israelites to accept Jesus the Messiah for what he is—the founder of the worldwide Heavenly Kingdom as God had originally intended and the leader of the world, a spiritual and political potentate.

Jesus failed to establish a living family of his own for personal restoration and the fulfillment of the four-position foundation. More important, he failed to unite the Israelites behind him. Jesus was not meant to die, he explained, contrary to what most Christians believed. Jesus died because of the failure of the Israelites to recognize him as their ruler. At this time God had the choice of keeping His son and forgetting humanity or sacrificing His son and keeping humanity as His own. He chose the latter. Satan then claimed the body of Jesus, while Jesus' spirit went to God and resided in Paradise until his mission is completed by somebody else on earth—at which time Jesus will be admitted to Heaven.

I listened hour after hour, fascinated by the consistency of the lectures. I was no biblical scholar, but the references seemed to fit so neatly—almost too neatly—into place in this system.

Moses spoke at great length about Jesus and the New Age. By Jesus' life, the price for worldwide spiritual indemnity was paid. All that remained was the setting of what the lecturer called the "Foundation of Substance," placing all economic matters under God's direct power through a new Messiah. The struggle to pave the way for this has resulted in all the major world conflicts since Jesus, including the great world wars, where God-centered democracy had to battle faithless satanic forces. Hitler was a par excellent example of the Antichrist, according to doctrine. I was shocked to hear Moses proceed to compare Hitler to Jesus. I was equally startled when Moses told us how we were now situated in the middle of World War III. The attempt to defeat godless communism with God-centered democracy is the test of man's foundation of substance. Particular nations have particular positions or roles in the struggle. Thus, America is in the archangel position of Satan, Japan is in the Eve position, and Korea is in the Adam position. Part of the duty of mankind is to protect and defend the Adam country, for this is third Israel and the land of the new Messiah. Because Korea is paving the way for the worldwide foundation on the national level, it should be the best loved and most respected nation on earth. All nations must humble themselves to Korea, the favorite nation in God's heart. And we all must be prepared for the Messiah, for He will come from this Eastern nation. He will not come in flowing robes, but as a modern man, to appeal to all men and women. Biblical astrology predicts that He was born between 1917 and 1922, that He is now roaming the earth, and that we must only find Him and follow. The audience laughed wildly as Moses chuckled: "And don't be surprised if He comes in a business suit!"

We sang and clapped, shouted hallelujah, our hearts on fire. The words took on an all-consuming power, filling us with hope, with new history, with a battery of slogans, and with an ideology to conquer the world for Heavenly Father. As Edie repeated at our group meeting, "Now that we have the Truth, nobody can stop us...."

eight/

I awoke on Friday with cotton mouth and dry tongue, exhausted from a night of disturbing restlessness. Who was I? Where was I? Was this the object of my search? Was this my God-chosen destiny, this special planned, predetermined mystical world where God gratefully accepted you for your suffering? And what about my swollen hand? Would God smile as my hand rotted off my arm, happy at my sacrifice?

My hand, hot and flaming, had swollen into a great mitt. As I touched each finger, I could see the oozing pus respond.

"God, dear God, save my hand! I've got to keep my hand!" I whispered. I ran outside, found Edie by the girls' trailer, and shouted frantically:

"Listen, Edie, I *demand* that somebody get me to a doctor right away. My hand has been infected for almost a week. I've had very little sleep here and no decent food and I can't fight the infection alone. Get me to a doctor this morning. I mean it!"

Edie looked at me crossly.

"Okay, okay, but don't act like such a spoiled little boy."

"Spoiled little boy? Because I'm angry, I'm a spoiled little boy? My God, what kind of a place is this?"

"Hush. Be quiet, Chris, or you'll disturb the others. C'mon with me."

We entered the trailer and Edie led me to Marilyn, a group member known for her acute telepathic powers and ability to read auras.

"Marilyn has to go to the doctor today. She'll take you."

"Now, now, what's wrong with this little boy?"

"Little boy! My God, I'm twenty-one years old."

"Come, come. What's the matter with our little boy?"

I blushed, embarrassed by her motherly tone.

"Look, Chris, you think you have trouble? Come here, take a look at my leg."

Marilyn rolled up her pants, revealing a giant gaping hole in her thigh. Black scabs competed to cover the horrible wound.

"That's what we mean by indemnity, Chris. I am paying for my sins and you are, too. You know Julian, the boy who worked with you on the crew? He prayed to accept responsibility for some of your sins. You know what happened to him? He's covered from head to foot with poison oak. It's a really awful case. You haven't been a good little boy all your life; I can tell, 'cause my spiritual senses are open. I can see, hear, and smell spirit world. And you know what? You smell bad. Phew! Your spiritual smell is awful. But you should smell Omma! Omma smells like spiritual roses. She's just beautiful, just like I always wanted my mother to be. But *she's* my mother now."

I had heard the name Omma mentioned casually by various Family members during the week. Perhaps Marilyn could tell me something about her.

"Who's Omma?"

"Omma? You haven't met Omma? You are really quite a little heavenly child, aren't you? Well, you'll meet her. And you'll agree, she's a heavenly sight to behold! She's the most beautiful woman I've ever met. And her spiritual power—it's tremendous! She tells us she speaks to Moses and Jesus all the time in spirit world and Heavenly Father gives her orders direct ... but you'll learn all of that in due time. Let's get back to that little swollen hand of yours."

I extended my hand. As she squeezed it, I cried out in pain.

"There, there, little boy. Everything will be all right."

I looked at her like a child seeking reassurance from his mother.

"Will it be all right?"

"There, there. The doctor will fix it right up. Just you wait and see."

She led me out to a battered '67 Valiant in the parking lot across the brook and we headed off toward the gate. The guard acknowledged her signal and waved her through. I looked around, seeking my bearings as the dilapidated vehicle careened around steep mountain curves.

"Marilyn, tell me about this Reverend Moon. What's he like?"

"Reverend Moon? Well, he's just the most wonderful man in the whole world. He's just the new Messiah, just the most important man to ever walk the earth. How did you hear about Reverend Moon? First-weekers aren't supposed to know about him."

"It's okay. Moses told me. He also told me about Reverend Moon's battle with Satan in spirit world. He told me about communism as Satan's greatest weapon in the world against God."

"Have you ever heard of 'Master Speaks,' Chris?" I sensed that Marilyn was cautiously feeling me out, trying to ascertain how much I knew or didn't know, how much she dared tell me.

"No. What's that?"

"That's Father's speeches. We call Reverend Moon Father, for he's the father of the universe. He's our father, our master, our lord. We are his servants, his children. Father is not only the nicest man in the whole world. He's also the smartest. Why, after years of prayer and struggle in spirit world, he's discovered all the great mysteries of history. His *Divine Principle* and 'Master Speaks' tell you everything you ever wanted to know about anything. It's an entire new way of looking at the world, Chris."

I gazed out the window as we entered a small anonymous town, drinking in the first signs of civilization I had seen in a week. I noticed a billboard, a picture of a man and woman lying on the beach, smoking Newports.

Marilyn noticed my gaze and said severely:

"Don't look at those things, Chris! That's Satan. He will attack you everywhere in the fallen world. That's why we keep locks on our gates at Boonville. It's to keep Satan and his work away from us. Don't you know? Everything around you is evil! Evil! There's only Heavenly Father and Satan and nothing in between. And now you're on Heavenly Father's side, you heavenly child, you!"

She reached over and pinched my cheek.

"So now you have to toss away your old life. All your thoughts, all your fantasies before the Family are *no good. No good! No good!* Out the window they go. Puff."

Marilyn rolled down the window and gestured as if to blow something out of her hand and into the wind. My hand was pulsating with pain now. A few minutes later Marilyn pulled into the hospital entrance, parked the car, reached for my unhurt hand to lead me in through the emergency room entrance.

I walked with her down the antiseptic corridor, filled with the strong smell of disinfectant. The walls and floors were immaculate. Everything looked so large! The people looked especially oversized, the same way they had looked when I could barely reach up to my mother's waist.

The receptionist was sitting at the switchboard, smoking a cigarette. How funny, I thought. How unnatural, I thought. How evil, I thought. Evil! Evil! Evil! The word reverberated through my mind. The surroundings seemed so alien to me, even though as a doctor's son I had been virtually raised in hospital waiting rooms and corridors.

90

While Marilyn conferred with the receptionist, I stared at the girl with my dilated pupils. Misinterpreting my gaze for a sexual advance, she fluffed her hair and leaned over, exposing a bare pink patch of breast. Satan! So he was here, too, just as they told me. Satan was everywhere, even in this innocent child. To my horror, I started to become aroused, but I squeezed my eyes and shouted within my mind: "Satan, get out! Satan, get out!" as they had taught me back on the farm. Then I cautiously opened my eyes, clenching one little fist.

"What's the matter, young man?" the girl asked.

"You, you, it's ... Oh, never mind. It's my hand. Look."

I raised my swollen hand, which by this time looked like a catcher's mitt. It throbbed terribly and I realized how frightened I was.

"Oh, my God! Dr. Strauss will have to look at that. Please go into that examining room, first door on your left."

Marilyn followed me into the antiseptic cubicle, where Dr. Strauss soon joined us. He reached for my hand, shook his head, and asked sharply: "How did you do this, son?"

"Oh, I was working on this farm in Boonville. I busted open the skin when I was swinging a pick."

"But why didn't you come in sooner, Chris? Do you realize what condition you're in? It looks like I may have to amputate."

Amputate? I knew it! I knew it was too late! Why hadn't anyone listened to me? Why hadn't they taken me to the hospital sooner? Now I would lose my hand! Or was this indemnity? Was I paying for my past sins? But I didn't want to lose my hand ... except perhaps for God. Maybe this suffering could be offered to Him as a holy gift. For God I would do anything.

Dr. Strauss, who had been carefully examining my wounds, peered at me over his glasses. "Chris, it looks like I may be able to save that hand after all. I think that if I can drain the pus, you may be all right with the help of an antibiotic. But you will have to promise to hold your hand up in the air when I finish so the wound will heal better."

"Uh, okay, sir." I gulped with relief.

The physician unwrapped a sterile scalpel, injected a local anesthetic, and began carefully slicing through the swollen flesh. The pain was excruciating, even with the anesthetic. I watched in horror and fascination as the blade split through the pulsating skin. Yellow-green fluid stained with blood flowed from the wound as he squeezed my hand. As it oozed down my palm, the surgeon skillfully wiped the festering mess away.

While Dr. Strauss finished his delicate procedure and wrapped my hand with gauze bandages, Marilyn told him about our wonderful Farm and invited him to dinner. He politely smiled, clearly not listening, and turned back toward me.

"You're a lucky guy. If you had come in twenty-four hours later, you would have certainly lost your hand. You've got to be more careful, son, and take better care of your body. There's just no excuse for your waiting this long before coming in."

The physician briefly looked at the infection on Marilyn's leg, changed the bandage, and placed her on new medication. He advised that she see him at his office next week for local surgery and told her to call for an appointment.

We thanked Dr. Strauss briefly, and Marilyn led me out of the room by my healthy hand. The anesthetic was already wearing off, and the pain was becoming unbearable, the worst I had ever experienced in my life. Instead of bearing up, I responded like a little child, crying bitter tears. As we sat on the grassy knoll outside the hospital, Marilyn hugged me, put my face to her breast.

"Now, now. Everything's going to be all right. Why, you're going to be some heavenly soldier, I can tell. What a brave boy you are, going all the way to the doctor practically by yourself."

When we reached the Valiant, I eagerly piled into the back seat, just as I used to do in my mother's station wagon. During the bumpy return ride, I leaned my chin on the back of the front seat. What a wonderful mother Marilyn was. What good care she took of her heavenly children.

I tried to keep my gaze fixed on back of Marilyn's head, for the world outside looked so filthy, so sinful. I noticed another billboard. The ad showed a picture of a luscious young woman in a black velvet dress, curled around a bottle of scotch. "Have you tried Black Velvet lately?" the sign asked. In spite of myself, I was drawn to the picture, to that wonderful womanly body.

"Chris, Chris, Satan is in you! I told you not to look at the signs. Satan is everywhere, tempting you. He wants you, 'cause you're such a valuable heavenly child. Satan really wants you, and God wants you, too. I think that you are the first Yalie God has rescued. You will have a very valuable mission, I'm sure. So keep yourself pure, follow your central figure in the Family, and you will grow into a glorious heavenly child. Why, I feel honored just to know you."

I beamed with pride. I suddenly flashed back to a scene at Yale, drudging away in the library, alone with no one to love me, no one who cared. How hungry I was for approval. How empty, how aching I felt in my heart ... How much I longed to be loved...

I sat back to think, struggling as Old Life feelings and New Life feelings battled within me.

I felt the need to give the Family values a better test, to experiment with them to see if they were as worthwhile as they seemed, but, much as I loved Marilyn and Edie and all the others, I still felt an urge to examine and reflect upon what had transpired over the past weeks. And so I made one last effort.

"Marilyn, I love you and all my friends on the Farm very much. But I think I should go away for a while to get another perspective."

"No, Chris. We won't let you go now. Too many people here love you. You're one of the most valuable people we've found. You are especially ripe for Satan's attacks. The more you doubt, the more Satan can magnify these doubts. You are so young in the Family, so vulnerable, Satan will actually get into your mind and possess you, control your every thought. Anyway, if you go back by train, Satan will derail the train. He's out to get you for sure. There's no doubt about it."

Silence. Her words left me confused and disoriented once more. I simply had to measure my old values against this new thinking, this heavenly thinking. And I couldn't do it here, I just couldn't. My head was swimming.

I was suddenly conscious again of the sharp nagging pain, dependent once more on Marilyn as a little child to his mom. Stop fighting it, Chris, my tired mind insisted. My mind whirred once again. A clear thought burst through the guarding barrier of vigilant new thought. At the same time, something within me cried: Chris, they can completely control you if they manage to limit your relationship to them through the role of the child. They destroy all your other roles, your identity as an individual, and they only allow the child to break through.

"Ohh, ahh, ahh." I moaned, utterly helpless in my predicament.

"Chris, Chris, don't get possessed now! Not while I'm driving! Listen to me, don't listen to your old satanic head. You must adopt New Age thinking entirely or you will be in danger of being destroyed. What's wrong with you, boy? Can't you see with your new spiritual glasses?"

I passively settled back in my seat. Too tired to think further, I began idly poking through some of the papers scattered about on the floor mat. Noting a manila envelope marked "Master Speaks," I eagerly picked it up, opened it, and began reading through the pile of pages, anxious to learn more about this mysterious prophet. It was a speech made by Reverend Moon in Seoul, South Korea, in 1975. As I turned the pages, my eyes widened. God and Satan, Communism versus Democracy, over and over in violent, repetitive phrases. He really spoke with the authority of a Messiah, I thought. What conviction! I was both frightened and impressed by each audacious announcement.

The speech grew stronger and stronger, building to a crescendo. Reverend Moon was inspiring the South Koreans to be vigilant, to prepare themselves for war! He spoke of the Unification Church in glorious tones as Korea's only hope in this war, as the world's only stronghold against communism. My heart started pounding as I read faster and faster.

Reverend Moon's urgent and militant tones jolted me. In the final paragraphs, he actually pledged Unification Church troops to fight with the South Korean Army against the North Koreans. *Unification Church troops!* Was this the love and peace group I was about to join? Fighting and killing? Was the new Messiah a warlord? Would I be trained to kill for God?

"Marilyn!"

"Yeah?"

"Marilyn, Reverend Moon really means business, doesn't he? I mean, we really are in a spiritual war, aren't we? He really wants to unite the world under his rule. These really are the Last Days, aren't they?"

"You're so right, Chris. These are the Last Days. And Heavenly Father's gonna be vic-torious. But don't worry about it. Just be obedient, grow in the Family and when you're strong enough, Father will have a mission for you. You're still such a spiritual baby. Just Ac-tualize the Principle. Be obedient to your subject, for each subject has a direct line to Father. Heavenly Father works through all the subjects in the Family. Surrender yourself completely to your subject, and Heavenly Father can prepare you for the Heavenly War. Yesssirree, these are the Last Days!"

I squirmed in my seat as we approached the gate to the farm. At a nod from Marilyn, the guard obediently opened the gate and we rumbled on down to the parking lot. As Marilyn cut the engine, I pulled on the door handle. In a flash, I was scampering back across the makeshift bridge to rejoin my new Family.

We had arrived just in time for the meditation hour. This was a daily ritual during which we were expected to maintain silence for an hour—a time to pray, take a shower, and write letters to family and friends. It was the one precious hour to think, to communicate with the outside world, to actually be yourself and make your own decisions free of outside influence of any kind.

I entered the shower house, stripped, and clustered among the bodies waiting to shower. Each naked body an honor, a glorious machine, a gift from God. I admired the skin, the muscles, the very flesh with which we were made. We existed as God's tool, I thought. What a fool I was not to have realized this earlier in my life! The body, the body an instrument of His increasing power. The legs, strong and sturdy, made to do God's work. The thighs, the key to physical motion. They radiated the glorious power of God's work. The genitals, God's servant to mankind, made to do the necessary work of procreation. The chest, the glorious chest which powers man by the power of breath. The arms, each arm a battle-ax, designed to defend God's Kingdom. The neck, designed to support the precious brain. The eyes, center of all spiritual power, for from the eyes radiates the joy that is the center of the universe. The nose, the mouth, the fingers, all these, I thought, were especially designed to play a part in God's command.

The shower shocked me with its icy coldness. Heaven's money could not be wasted on anything so trivial as heat. I noticed one young man standing under the freezing spray with a look of supreme pleasure on his face. He had been standing under the shower since I first entered, stock still, staring out into space, sporting a tremendous grin. I nudged Keith, who was drying off next to me, and asked in a whisper what this brother was doing.

"Oh, he's an older brother. He's doing a shower condition. He's doing it for indemnity, suffering for his sins for God. Remember what Moses said about indemnity? It's the cornerstone of the *Divine Principle*. Wait till you have heard the lectures two or three times. They'll begin to sink in after a few weeks. We must all maintain a prayerful attitude toward God and pay Him back for our sins through our suffering. Don't worry, you'll be doing it, too. God knows what's best for you. He'll guide you through your suffering. You will be so grateful that you are a heavenly child that you'll do just anything for God."

I walked out of the shower room, astonished. Were these people on some sort of masochistic trip? Or were they really working for God? Were these the rules of the universe, that God should accept such pain in the war against Satan?

How could I judge truth? I felt my old standards were clearly inadequate. But without any old standards, how could I judge new ones? I had pledged to Edie that I would try the new ways, so I must try to follow center and pay close attention to what my older brothers and sisters did and ordered me to do. I must not judge so harshly, I thought. What if God were really grateful enough for a cold shower to accept us as His children? What if He could really claim this allegiance for Himself in the battle against Satan?

I left the shower room house, wearing the crumpled old clothes I had pulled out of the collective laundry hamper. Looking across the green, I saw Sam wearing my checkered shirt, Bill wearing the sweater I had bought before heading for California. All our clothes were thrown together and we dressed on a first-come, first-serve system, those newest in the Family choosing the shabbiest clothes to show humility and Family leaders picking out the finest as a sign of their status.

With a half hour of meditation period left, I sat down under a tree to write my first letter since arriving on the farm, a brief message to a college friend. As I wrote, older brothers greeted me quietly, smiling, patting me on the back as they passed. If this wasn't the Heavenly Kingdom . . .

Dear Ryan,

I have met something quite spectacular on my visit to California. I have found a spiritual group called Creative Community Projects. It's an educational and religious group. The spiritual standards are of the highest order. Shunning all drugs, sex, and selfish pleasure, the group stresses spiritual development. The group is a very enthusiastic one. We exist to bring love and joy to the community around us. The people here are really great. Their very presence makes me high.

I still have many questions to ask here. I don't know what I will do with my life, but I do plan to stay here for now. I plan to check this community out thoroughly. It seems to fill all the standards I was looking for but never found at Yale. I have met spiritual, loving people, many of whom were mysteriously and directly guided to this place.

I plan to write you again, to share my thoughts and feelings. We are allowed an hour each day, an hour of silence to reflect and write letters. I will keep you posted on how I am growing in my new beautiful home.

> Best,
> Chris

"Tweeeeee." At the sound of the whistle marking the end of the hour, all the brothers piled out onto the lawn. I followed and we all lined up in front of the girls' trailer. Today Timmy led the group. He had shared with the Family earlier, describing himself as an ex-eco freak, an ecology fanatic who had fled to the wilds of Alaska to bury his frustrated idealism in the Arctic snows. But his sister joined the Family three years ago and sent him a very convincing letter about her new community, so he hitched to California to return to civilization. Judging from his beaming face, he seemed to have found the ready acceptance and love he sought in the Family.

"Okay, brothers!" he shouted. "Hey, yay, great day! Is everybody happy?"

"Yes!" we all chanted in unison.

"Is everybody in-spired?"

"Yes!" we all cried.

"Then, brothers, let's call for the sisters to get to their heavenly work. At the count of three: oh—sisters! One, two, three."

"Oh—Sisters!" we shouted.

One sister leaped out of the trailer, did a little dance. Twenty-five other women marched out and lined up like Israeli soldiers preparing for war.

"Okay, brothers and sisters, what are we going to do?"

"Work!"

"I can't hear you. What are we going to do?"

"Work!"

"Louder!"

"Work!"

"Now, that's more like it."

Jimmy read off the list of workers and where each individual was supposed to go. I raised my arm as the doctor had ordered.

"What do you want, brother?"

"Oh, nothing."

"Then why are you raising your hand, brother?"

"Because my doctor told me to."

"Well, put it down, brother. That's not how we work things around here."

Timidly, I complied.

"Who here is a first-weeker?" Jimmy demanded.

About twenty-five hands shot up.

"Okay, first-weekers. You're on ground crew. We're going to do some really heavenly work today...."

I waved my arm in the air.

"*Now* what do you want, brother?"

"Well, brother, I can't use my right hand. My doctor told me not to use it."

"Okay, brother, then how 'bout if we put you in with the *sisters?* You can make some nice oatmeal cookies for the weekend. All right, everybody fall in! That's it, be good heavenly soldiers. Now, somebody from each group go get the songbooks. I want to hear you really sing this afternoon. Get goin'."

nine/

As brooms were dispensed to sweep the Chicken Palace for the coming busload of weekend guests, I realized that it was the end of my first full week on the Farm. This came as a shock; evidence that I was losing grasp of time in this new world-without-watches, this world shaped by good-morning songs, whistles, and evening choo-choos on the lawn.

Lectures on the Fall of Man, the failures of Jesus, the sinfulness of the Israelites, the new understanding of human history—these had all been drilled into me hour after hour. By this point, I had passed the stage of questioning and entered a stage of acceptance, for in this tightly controlled environment there was no room for debate. Our whole purpose was to memorize Reverend Moon's mysterious revelations. During my first seven days on the farm I never once heard a Family member doubt or express any personal interpretation of anything. Whenever I commented on this, I would receive the same reply: "Well, Truth is Truth," repeated over and over by various group members in exactly the same fashion.

Every time I tested the group's philosophy, I saw it eagerly embedded in the hearts and minds of believers. After a week of being prodded, provoked, and carefully watched, I had learned that the key to induction into the Family was to literally subjugate the spirit, to conquer for God. Once I fully accepted this principle, I was eager to practice this form of control over other people, imitating the people who were subjugating me.

During this time, my spiritual father, Jacob, had sent me two promised gifts from the city—a Baby Ruth bar and a blank notebook — which delighted me no end, as though God himself had come down on the clouds and handed me the candy. How could I, worthless me, receive such treasures from such a righteous person? How could I possibly be entitled to a chunk of the Heavenly Kingdom? At first I viewed the Heavenly Kingdom as a possibility to be tested, but as the week progressed I began to accept it much more literally. I embraced what I wanted to believe so badly, the chance to live for something I could die for, to live and die for a love eternal, a love so strong that by its own whim it could command life or death.

I wanted to believe that I had permission to sacrifice all my hopes and dreams into the existing belief system, and people around me kept reinforcing this by praising me, making me feel valuable as a reborn person, promising me the sky.

During that first week while working on the trail I had learned that there were other farms like this across the country.

"Are they all controlled by the same people?" I asked Jim.

"Of course. Reverend Moon will soon be the most powerful man in America. All our other farms are officially acknowledged to be part of the Unification Church. We call this one by a different name to attract people in Berkeley because people would never show up for dinner if they thought we were a religious group."

So there was more to the Family than one little magical farm where God guarded His secrets! Maybe I could actually make a change in the world, as I had once dreamed and Family members constantly promised.

For the last few days I had been paying particularly close attention to the "more spiritual" Family members like Marilyn. These were the people I wanted to investigate, for they seemed to have some special God-given powers. Marilyn, for example, not only read auras for people, but she picked up on people's vibrations and claimed to be able to read minds. She gave her life testimony at a Family dinner that Friday evening after lecture:

"My dearest Family, I want to share my past with you. As a child, I was always considered special. If I picked up a spoon, I could feel tiny vibrations. I knew the spoon was alive, with a special being of its own. I soon began to see auras, colorful emanations around peoples' heads. By these auras, I could judge a person's character, tell whether he or she was in some sort of danger."

Marilyn explained that her parents took her to mediums to try to understand this power. A medium told her she was gifted by God, chosen for some special mission. By the time she was thirteen, people all over town would consult her, asking for mediumistic readings. When she fell into a trance, her guide, a departed spirit named Fowler, would speak through her.

"I gradually learned that through Fowler I could heal sick people by placing my hands on their forehead and concentrating on changing their vibrations."

One day, Marilyn told us, she was doing a reading for somebody when Fowler began to speak directly to her. He told her that she was being prepared for a very special mission. "He told me that I would soon meet a very beautiful Korean lady." This lady would give Marilyn spiritual guidance and direct her and Fowler would soon leave her. And that was the last time that she ever heard Fowler's voice.

We sat up on our knees, our ears perked in anticipation.

"Later, my Family, at the end of that week, I was strolling along the Berkeley campus, when I suddenly felt a

103

magnetic attraction." Marilyn followed it and found herself standing under a sign that read Creative Community Projects. Sitting under the shade of a nearby tree was "our beloved Omma." Omma pointed to Marilyn, beckoned, and asked if she wanted salvation. "I couldn't resist the power in her eyes and I knew I was conquered by her love." Older members nodded and smiled knowingly at each other.

Omma took her packages, held her by the hand, and led her through the streets of Berkeley to a small apartment. There, over dinner, she explained to her new friend the *Divine Principle* in her English-Korean accent.

Marilyn told us that she was spellbound. She rushed back for dinner the next night and the night after that. Each night Omma would feed her, pamper her, treat her like the lost little girl she was. "I knew upon hearing the talks that she was teaching me divine secrets."

Marilyn's eyes lit up as she described the amazing power of Omma's love. By the end of the week, Marilyn knew that she was conquered for God. "What a wonderful feeling it was, having the protection and guidance of this new mother of mine."

She concluded by saying that in the Family she can put her spiritual powers to good use for Heavenly Father. She can grow closer to God with all her loving brothers and sisters.

The fifty people crammed in the little trailer suddenly whistled and burst into simultaneous applause. Everyone was smiling, grinning from cheek to cheek, delighted by Heavenly Father's power. Marilyn sat down, beaming. We all dug into our squash, bean, and salad dinner as Moses, at the center of the circle, called on another person to give testimony.

I could feel myself getting high, high from this smiling group, this happy Family surrounding me. Whatever my doubts might be, it seemed that this loving circle must have an element of goodness. And if there is goodness, then mustn't it be true?

The testimonies continued on into the night. After the main course was finished, the cooks brought out giant portions of ice cream, served every Friday night on the farm amid shouts of joy. I participated self-consciously at first, but gradually came to enjoy the role of little child they had given to me. The burden of responsibility for judging the Principle had at last been lifted from me. I forgot the many questions I had had about the previous lecture, consumed in this controlled expression of joy.

"Individual Entertainment" followed. Various members of the audience volunteered to sing selections out of the songbook on an impromptu stage. What innocent joy, this entertainment was, I thought, a great way for guests to release their inhibitions and prove themselves to older members. Mary stood up and sang "Go Down, Moses." Keith, as an older member, sang a more militant song of self-righteousness, "Marching on, Heavenly Soldiers." The crowd cheered frantically. Edie, who was keeping close tabs on me as usual, elbowed me.

"What, Edie?"

"Well, aren't you going to sing? You're the only second-weeker who hasn't sung."

"I am?"

"Sure. Now, go sing."

"No thanks. I don't care to."

"Go. Go do what you're told."

"No. C'mon, Edie, I don't want to."

Phil, overhearing the conversation, collapsed in prayer behind me to ask for the salvation of my soul. I could feel my face grow hot. No one had ever prayed for me before, let alone for God to forgive me for not singing. Maybe I just had a lot to learn about the way in which God works...

"Don't be such a spoiled child, Chris," Edie persisted. "Now, come on, do what I tell you. It's for your own good. And remember, if you want to grow in the Family you have to follow center. Come on, are you afraid of what people will think of you? Are you really afraid?"

Me—afraid? I'd never thought of it that way. It looked like I'd have to prove to her that I wasn't and that I wanted to be part of this Family.

"What should I sing?"

"Sing something that indicates your rebirth as a heavenly child. Sing something you'd never sing in Old Life."

As she said Old Life, Edie wrinkled her nose. She paged through the songbook, paused to think, tugged my shirt. "Sing 'God Bless America.' Go on!"

No, I could never sing that song. My God, I had been so ashamed of my country, a country consumed by worship of the dollar and aggrandizement of the self. What would my leftist college friends think if they saw me now? But since that was the most difficult song to sing of all, I decided I'd have to do it to prove to myself that I could, that I could even become a heavenly child if I wished. Edie raised my hand, and Moses called on me. I stood up and walked over to the stage.

"God Bless America—Land that I love ..." I began in a choked voice. An image flashed across my mind. I was nine years old, at a baseball game with my brother and Dad. A scratchy record was playing the National Anthem as the Yankees paused from their pregame warm-up. I felt the same lump in my throat that I was feeling now.

As I continued, singing louder, my voice cracked with emotion. My hands trembled. Everyone was staring at me, trying to establish eye contact, looking completely transfixed in typical Family fashion. My voice trembled and I began to choke again as I spilled out the faintly remembered words.

My eyes began to water. Another image appeared. I was at home, with my grandmother, probably four years old. I sat there in my jammies, the Doctor Denton's with little leather feet, watching TV with my Nana as the station was signing off. A flag appeared on the screen as the National Anthem was sung. The image faded, to be replaced by yet another one. Kate Smith was on *The Ed Sullivan Show*, dressed in a black spangled dress. She was belting out her famous version of "God Bless America" to millions of Sunday night viewers, shaking her vast body, squeezing the microphone in her chunky hands. Kate was working up a storm. Streams of tears built up in my eyes, gathering at the lids, blurring the sea of eager faces.

"God bless America—My home sweet home!"

The audience rose in unison, breaking into frenetic applause. Two brothers picked me up, led me around the room, and dropped me off next to an ecstatic Edie. Tears streamed down my face, tears of joy or sadness, or God knows what in this chaotic caldron of unbridled emotion.

I was a little child once again, the child who cried when Tarzan slipped from his vine or Lois Lane got captured by crooks. The Family kept jostling me, elbowing me, shaking my hand. Nobody had ever loved me so much, nobody had really cared.... This was where I wanted to stay, where I could be loved and accepted. This was the place where God wanted me to be....

the heavenly kingdom

ten/

I kneaded the dough with my fingers, working the thick paste. My hand, now bandaged securely, was able to handle the sticky mixture safely. Together with Janie, a first-weeker with long, blond braids and an innocent look, I was preparing cookies for the evening meal. As a second-weeker, going on a third-weeker, I naturally felt it was my duty to initiate this newcomer.

"You know, Janie, I've only been in the Family for two weeks, but I've decided to stay for a while. I've never seen so much love anywhere in my life. And the Principles ... Well, I don't know if they're all true but I'm certainly going to check them out. I hope you'll decide to settle here, as I have. Why, God is in the trees and bushes here. God's even here in the cookie dough!"

I pushed my fingers up through the malleable dough, my hand emerging to wave hello to Janie. She looked startled, then we both laughed. I smiled to myself. My calculated use of body language had lured her, eased her fears, appealed to the sensuality that radiated from her round little body. Her pupils widened in response as her arms pushed slowly through the heavy dough.

Marilyn had entered the room in time to witness my tactics. She nodded to me approvingly, leaned over, and whispered, "You're really learning the ropes, Chris. But just be sure that after you subjugate her with your love you guide her well. You really shouldn't be doing this of course; it's what spiritual parents do to their children. But it's good for you to practice your psychic powers. They sure do come in handy!" We both smiled while Janie stared trancelike into the cookie dough. I passed my hands over hers and dug into the goopy stuff. She eagerly followed, actively imitating my every gesture. I sensed that her spirit was becoming as docile and pliable as the dough that oozed through our fingers.

"God made our bodies to comply with definite physical and spiritual laws. Here's how someone who loves God should knead dough." I dug in once again, gracefully churning the dough with soft, circular motions. My hand twisted at the wrists, making giant arcs. Janie gazed at me, mystified, like a small child staring at a trapeze act in a circus show. I knew I had her now. This was my first capture, my first victory for Heavenly Father in the system that had conquered me. I had been trapped by Satan's world, so now I had to be trapped for God, or so I had been taught. I now lived to convert, to reproduce in others what had taken place in me. I was a good heavenly child. I was a good heavenly...

"*Tweeeeee!*" The whistle told me it was time to stop work and prepare for lecture. I shaped the remaining dough into balls, placed them on buttered trays, and popped them in the oven. People were running by, eager to "Circle Up" in the brothers' trailer. Since I had heard today's lecture several times before, I decided to stay behind and finish my baking. Renee hurried past, turned, and ran back toward me.

"And what do you think you're doing, little boy?"

"Well, uh, I'm finishing the cookies."

"Oh no you don't. You're still a baby. You need to hear the lecture to sharpen your faith. Look, I'm going, and I've heard this lecture at least a hundred times. Anyway, you never even checked with Edie. Remember, she's your subject, your center person whom you must obey without question. Chris, you're too stubborn and independent. Before you can become heavenly, you have to be a good object for your center man. Now, come on. I'll send Sheri in to finish the cookies. Hurry! They're already singing. Let's go!"

Renee grabbed my hand and pulled me toward the glass door. Why did I have to hear the lecture again? Why? Why? Why? As we entered the brothers' trailer, Edie motioned for us to join our group. During the next fifteen minutes we ran through five songs, starting out slowly and softly working up to a frenzied crescendo. As we swayed back and forth in our circle, arms on each other's shoulders, we gazed deep into each other's eyes. By studying the older members of the Family, I had learned how they used their gaze to subjugate younger members. I turned to a confused first-weeker at my side, penetrating her eyes with the force within mine, then "sending" her focus of consciousness to another older Family member by shifting my gaze from her eyes to theirs. She automatically followed suit, her gaze directed by mine. What an effective trick this was! I noticed that a number of other group members were using the same technique. After all, wasn't any method fair that encouraged group unity? Wasn't the most important thing to gain the new members' trust, to draw them closer to the older members, to bring them nearer to God, Who spoke to them directly through the lecturer?

By the time the singing ritual was over, the group was bursting with energy, like human batteries, filled with a spiritual high that comes from "melting together like marsh-mallows," as Edie called it—an emotional high that virtually obliterates thought.

We all sat down on cue, younger members taking out their notebooks as older members bowed in prayer for the conversion of their guests. I found the notebook Jacob had given me, once filled with questions and misunderstandings. But now I took it out to copy every word of the lecture, to learn it all by heart. After all, this was God speaking through Moses.

As I looked around the room, I thought about how

worthless, how undeserving I was, what a sinner I had been all my life, how unworthy to communicate with such holy people. Edie and Renee on my right and left were checking to make certain that I was writing in my notebook, examining every word I put down on the page.

Moses launched into an explanation of how the world had failed Jesus, how the Israelites rejected him, how even John the Baptist failed him in his hour of need. Half the audience, largely Jewish by birth, was wracked with tears. Moses writhed in agony as he retold the story of the crucifixion. Older members gazed into his eyes, as he spoke, believing they could return God's love energy to Moses by beaming it back upon him. Others in the audience bowed their heads, dried the tears from their eyes, and prayed to God for forgiveness.

For the last few days, I had been encouraged not to approach the lectures intellectually. Edie had told me time and again to listen "heartfully," to let my feelings come out, to let God talk to me directly. Today, as Moses moaned about the suffering of Jesus, I felt a sharp pain in my side, a heavy pressure on my chest, although nobody was touching me. I began to cry, my fists rolled up into balls. In order to hide my tears, I walked to the back of the room and turned around, only to see Moses staring at me. Moses was accusing me; God was accusing me!

In the back of the room, I continued to listen to Moses, but my pain increased. Clutching my heaving stomach, I whispered, "My God, why do I have to endure such suffering? Is this the type of suffering Jesus spoke about, the kind he willingly accepted as payment for our sins?" I suddenly leaned forward as foul-tasting fluid filled my cheeks. My whole body began to tremble. I quietly tried a relaxation exercise to gain control over myself, arching my back, then throwing my head forward. The pain temporarily stopped. As I leaned back, my eyes rolled into my head. I recovered, looked down the aisle toward the lectern, and there was Moses, writing furiously on the blackboard, shouting at the top of his voice:

"But now Jesus is dead and God is dead and the Creation is dead. We failed Jesus, dear sweet Jesus, and his loving Father, the Lord our God. God had the choice of saving His favorite son and letting humanity perish in Satan's hands or sacrificing His son so you and I could be saved. He was crucified for us and Satan claimed his body, wracked and tortured.

"So God asks once again that you follow Him, that you be prepared to follow His words. Join the Family, come back to God and be saved, join the crusade for the Lord of the Second Advent...."

I began to weave back and forth, my body revolving from the hips. Suddenly, in an ecstatic fit I raised my hands and lowered them, bowing to Moses. I was losing myself, swept away in this frenzy, just like the rest of the audience.

Moses abruptly stopped his lecture and bowed his head. I joined the others in a woeful hymn, sharing my book with an older brother. As he wiped his nose with a checkered handkerchief, he hugged me in a brotherly way. Perhaps this was the place where I could become a pure gift for God, I thought once again. I looked at my beautiful brother here, moved to tears by his compassion and humanity.

"Glory to God in the highest. Peace on earth, goodwill toward men."

As we settled down, Moses closed with a prayer:

"Our dearest Heavenly Father, we thank You for the gift of life You give us, we, your undeserving children. We have failed You, time and time again. Yet—" (Moses sobbed)— "You sent us Jesus to save us. And we failed him. Lord, Lord, when You send another prophet for us, help us to not be so blind that we don't recognize him. We pray most humbly in our Master's name. Amen."

The group slowly filed out of the trailer and into their small meeting circles. The chilly night air grabbed us and sent us shivering—teeth chattering, goose bumps popping up on arms. In spite of the cold, nobody mentioned sweaters or jackets for fear of seeming selfish. Edie led me toward her circle by the hand, speaking to me as we walked:

"Chris, I could see that you were quite moved by the lectures. You're such a spiritual person, so open and sensitive. You're going to be a very strong brother, very brave and courageous. But repent, repent, I warn you. Repent, or Satan will take you away from us. Follow center and throw those concepts of yours away. No more concepts. No more concepts. Now, I want you to write it on your hand like this, see." She wrote on the palm of my hand with her Bic pen: NO MORE CONCEPTS. I stared at the slogan blankly. It was appealing in a strange sort of way, a refreshing release from my past, the many years when questioning and answering yielded only more confusion and despair. "No more concepts." I repeated it slowly in my mind over and over, savoring those precious words. As I broke into a broad smile, Edie giggled with delight.

"Brothers and sisters, I have an announcement to make," Edie shouted: "Through patient effort and heavenly perseverance, Chris has finally abandoned his old life. Chris is Reborn! Let's hear it! Re-born. Re-born."

Everybody chanted in unison: Re-born. Re-born. Chris is Re-born." We all held hands, swinging arms back and forth, mechanically following Edie's example. She and some of the older Family members immediately burst into song. "We love you, Chri-i-is, oh yes we do ... We love you, Chri-i-is, and will be true. When You're not wi-ith us, we're blue ... Oh, Chri-i-is, we love you!" I blushed, embarrassed, yet touched by the childish lyrics, by the group's attention. Those loving, smiling faces ... This really must be the Heavenly Kingdom.

"Yes, boys and girls, Chris is reborn. And in the Family people can be reborn every weekend. You die to the old self to bring forth the new person, the person of the New Age. Brothers and sisters, I think Chris has something to tell us."

I blushed again and smiled sheepishly, rehearsing in my mind a proclamation I had heard from others countless times.

"Brothers and sisters, I announce tonight my intention to stay and live with the Family forever. This is where I belong, a place to teach and learn and a place to love one another. Before I joined the Family I was worthless, no good—I drank, I smoked, I had feelings toward women. I was a rebel, a scavenger, a parasite. But all that's behind me now. I can forget the past. I am reborn. Hooray for Heavenly Father and hooray for the Heavenly Kingdom!"

The group burst into shouts and cheers. Several brothers shook my hand, slapped me on the back. Even the two confused first-weekers in the group joined in the raucous celebration. I rocked back and forth, consumed with joy. Where, O God, were you all my life? Why had I been so stubborn, how could I have been so far from You?

Edie addressed the group, "Okay, brothers and sisters. There's time for applause, there's time for laughter. But there's also a time for repentence. We failed Jesus. We in the Family represent the past seven generations of our physical family. They worked so hard to bring us to the Family. They had to work so hard because they failed Jesus. And we failed Jesus, too, since we represent our physical families. We must not just forget the past. We must respect the universal law of indemnity, the law of suffering and repentence which is the cosmic road to salvation. We mūst follow our central figure to the letter, to obediently comply, to humble our spirits to our leader, especially since we failed our first leader, Jesus. When Jesus came, it was his mission to serve mankind. With the advent of the Lord of the Second Coming, the new Messiah's reign on earth, it is humanity's mission to serve the Messiah. When Jesus died, he entered Paradise. With the coming of the second Messiah, even Jesus is a suffering servant of this new Messiah, working night and day in spirit to usher in the Lord of the Second Advent."

"Rejoice, the Lord is here! Rejoice, the Lord is here! Rejoice, the Lord is here!" several members chanted in unison. I joined in eagerly, glad to be a part of the group. "Rejoice, the Lord is here! Rejoice, the Lord is here! Rejoice, the Lord is here!" I belonged someplace at last; I was free to express my joy, free to touch a brother or sister with innocence. I was totally happy and free for the first time in my life. God, thank You. Jesus, thank you. I clutched Edie's arm, cupped my hand to her ear, and whispered, "Edie, I think

Heavenly Father's calling me. I feel the need for deep, repentful prayer, the first such prayer of my life. May I please be excused to go pray?"

"Why, certainly, brother. Just be sure to come back before we meet in the large Family circle by the fire."

"Okay, Edie."

"And, Chris. One more thing. Heavenly Father loves you." As she said "you," she dramatically pushed her finger into my chest.

I stood up and scooted off toward the hills, like a schoolboy on a grade school hike, the chilly wind ripping through my thin plaid shirt as I ran. Skipping over to my favorite spot, where the lapping waters sang the praises of God, I knelt in prayer, resting my elbows on the damp, hard earth, hands clasped together on my forehead.

"Dearest Heavenly Father," I murmured. "Thank You for answering my prayers. Thank You for guiding me to the Family. Forgive me for, for killing Jesus, forgive me for not following him as the Second Adam, forgive me Lord, for, for cru-cifying him!" With this I burst into tears, blubbering and wiping my nose with my sleeve. A sudden blast of wind rushed up the legs of the old patched pair of army surplus pants I had pulled from the clothes bin that morning.

"Forgive me, Lord, for my ancestors. And forgive me for myself, for I am the sum total of sins of my ancestors. Forgive me for mocking Jesus, for making fun of the crucifix-ion. Heavenly Father, Lord of all, grant me one wish. Please, Father, work to make me forget my past, my foolish, sinful past. Give me a new identity. Give me a new name if You wish. But, Heavenly Father, if You can grant me one wish, grant me this wish. Help me put a distance between my past and my present, to forget my education, forget my family, forget all my foolish deeds. Please, please help me to forget myself. And mold me into a new and more righteous person. And forgive me, Lord, for those foolish deeds of my past. In Master's name I pray. Amen."

On the way back to the group I noticed a figure crouched on the opposite bank of the brook. It was a member of Marilyn's group, a highly sensitive woman who had been having numerous spiritual experiences since she met the Family. Shaking and swinging her fists violently in the air, she was swiping at imaginary demons, as she screamed:

"Get thee behind me, Satan! Get thee behind me! Get thee behind me, Satan! Get thee behind me!"

In the distance I saw three groups sitting in circles on the open ground, on grass burned to yellow straw by the blazing summer sun. Hand in hand, they shook their arms up and down to the sound of the Family chant: "Choo-choo-choo, choo-choo-choo, choo-choo-choo. Yay, yay — Pow!" Over and over they shouted, louder and louder, faster and faster. And in the background Marilyn's charge continued to berate Satan.

As I stumbled along the path, the seriousness of my new commitment suddenly struck me. I had entered another new world, a Brave New World of sorts, and there would be no way out. The screaming, the love-bombing, the tears, and, most of all, the new Heavenly thinking ... Was I strong enough, was I pure enough? Could I fight away the "old thoughts" that kept plaguing me, telling me that this was just structured madness? Yet I knew from the lectures that Heavenly Father couldn't accept me until I accepted Him.... From here, there can be no going back. No going back. Ever...

By the end of my third week on the farm, my mind had been swept clean of doubt, a whitewashed wall, a clean tablet to be scribbled upon at will. I confessed my total dependence upon the group, which I allowed to regulate all my eating and sleeping habits; they told me when I could and couldn't go to the bathroom, directed me when to pray and when to talk, or be still, when to laugh and when to cry. I was told when I could act up, when I could be a child and play as a child, when I should act mature, how I should appear to new members. I ... I who had learned to live alone, to dwell in solitude, I who had been free to create any life I wished. I was now learning to live in utter conformity—no, utter obedience to the demands of my peers. I was reduced to nothing, a new heavenly child, with no past life, no history.

One afternoon during meditation hour I walked past a line of men outside the brothers' trailer. They were waiting for Edie, who stood in front of a brother seated on a folding chair. She was busy snipping the long locks and beard of the second-weeker. His shoulder-length hair dropped to the ground, as Edie cut and cut, until only a few inches of bristle remained. The lumberjack beard, which he had carefully grown for over a year with such pride, was suddenly reduced to clippings in the massive pile of hair surrounding the chair. He stood up and smiled as the Family ritual was completed. Several sisters ran over to him immediately and whispered, "Oh, you look so-oo handsome!" I remembered how happy I had been one week earlier as I enjoyed this new transition into Family life.

I sat down under a large tree and opened the diary book Jacob had given me. Perhaps reading my notations would help me retrace the path I had taken, remind me of the nature of my search.

"This diary is dedicated to laying the groundwork for the unity of science and religion," I read. My first entry was an essay, a discourse on the nature of science. The next entry was a list of questions, 126 questions I had asked about the group, 37 of which had never been answered.

Once again, I picked up a pencil and entered my thoughts in tiny letters. Summing up the essence of my relationship to God and world, I scrawled:

The smaller I am, the greater it is.
The greater it is, the smaller I am.
The greater it is, the greater I am.
The greater I am, the greater it is.
The greater I am, the smaller I am.
The smaller I am, the greater it is.

eleven/ I saw hundreds of people come
and go during those first weeks on the farm, watched streams
of newcomers react to the constant joyful singing and the
lavish dose of attention administered to each "Boonville
Baby," a term the older members cynically used when secretly joking to each other about a newcomer. Out of these
hundreds of guests, about eighty-five to a hundred stayed on
working on trails and in the fields with the veterans, learning
the "Heavenly Way." Class distinctions seemed to be erased
on the farm as fundamentalists from midwestern Bible col-
leges, black southern Baptists, northeastern intellectuals, and
cowboys chatted like brothers and sisters. Everything appeared as it should be, except for occasional complaints about
the heavy regimentation, which were usually squelched
immediately and tactfully.

When I once remarked about the regimentation to
Moses, he explained to me:

"New members always balk a bit about the structure. They don't understand the heavenly way of life. But once they hear the lectures and work for a few weeks, they calm down and accept all the rules. When they finally embrace the Principle, they don't need laws or rules at all—they just obey God!"

I grew to understand that once on the farm, which older members frankly called "Training Center," each person internalized Family rules until there was no longer any need for training. I was told that at that point, new members were shipped to the city to work for the Heavenly Kingdom, and Edie promised me that very soon, when my own training was complete, I would get to work for God, too. If older members "burned up" from too much constant work or if they seemed to forget the rules, they were immediately sent back to the Farm to become recharged and retrained. The word "indoctrination" flashed through my mind, but I repressed such thoughts by thinking that one needs this drastic treatment to withdraw completely from the fallen world, open himself up to new thought, and confess his ultimate dependence upon people. After all, it wasn't *easy* to be Re-born....

New members usually left for the city after their third or fourth week, depending on how heavenly they had become — how well they had internalized the rules. I gradually learned the unwritten rules for leaving the farm from all my older brothers and sisters:

1. Give all your attention to the lecturer when he lectures. Stare him straight in the eyes. When somebody starts to fall asleep, knock him squarely in the forehead or massage his back.

2. Sing as loudly and enthusiastically as possible. This is part of what everybody on the farm called "giving one-oh-oh," or 100 percent. Sing as if God can listen to your loving song.

3. Work to inspire or arouse your neighbor, no matter how many doubts or questions you may have. "Everything must be elevating" is the common phrase, one of about a hundred phrases that travel through the group continuously.

Always be conscious of the needs of your brothers and sisters, working exclusively upon attaining their salvation by conversion. Love them so much that they'll never want to leave.

4. Learn how to work over the younger members, to subjugate them with your love, to control them through your gestures. This works in conjunction with unwritten rule three, for you control your neighbor when you make him sufficiently depressed about his past and the condition of the world and make him as high as possible for his present and future life in the Family. Feed them with despair, then hit 'em with hope, their only hope—the Family.

After listening to older members praise Family life for the past few weeks, I was eager to Ac-tualize in the city. I wanted to work with the Family on their various "business projects," and I wanted to bring other people to the group by proselytizing, a phenomenon called "witnessing to the Truth." Older Family members enticed me with tales of how wonderful it was to work in the city. They said it was "real pioneering." I was eager for the hard stuff after my time on the Farm. I thought I was well-enough trained, spiritual enough now to try my wings in the city. Marilyn told me, "You must go to the city if you want to grow. There you'll really grow quickly." So I decided to try extra hard during my fourth weekend to impress Edie with my readiness to move on.

Seven o'clock on Saturday morning rolled around quickly. The new members who had arrived from the city would be awakened soon, so I scurried outdoors with the rest of the brothers and sisters to begin our day before the guests were jarred awake by good-morning songs. We gathered firewood and built a fire in the middle of the campground. I then joined a work crew going out into the fields and picked tomatoes for an hour. With the sound of the whistle, we returned to the campsite to meet our new brothers and sisters, who were busy investigating their new surroundings. There were at least 130 people in the three-stall bathroom, and some brother had borrowed and misplaced my toothbrush. We piled out of the bathroom at the sound of another whistle and shouts of "Exercise time, exercise time!" After running through the usual twenty minutes of calisthenics, we launched into a musical "Simon Says." I sang along with the others as guests including bearded social scientists and eminent young theologians shook their posteriors in a circle to the tune of "Hokey-Pokey."

David, the leader of the exercises, then assigned us to our appropriate groups. I was placed in Edie's group as usual. On my way to my circle, Lottie, an older Family member I had met on my first weekend, came over and pinched my cheek.

"Hello, heavenly child. I didn't think you'd make it this far. You were asking too many questions that first week. In fact, I heard you were one of our most difficult cases to crack. It took a lot of prayer and hard work to get you here and convert you. Congratulations, little boy!"

She shook both of my hands. Suddenly, she burst out with a "Choo-choo-choo, choo-choo-choo, choo-choo-choo. Yay, yay — Pow!" She then flashed a gleaming smile and skipped off like a little elf into her own group.

Our group gathered together, and Edie told Renee and me to fetch breakfast. When we returned with jugs of chocolate milk and granola, I carefully placed the first portion, intended for Heavenly Father, in front of my center person, Edie. Edie drew me aside as the group launched into "Oh, What a Beautiful Morning" and showed me a card bearing the names of our weekend guests. Arrows indicated which Family members had been secretly assigned to each newcomer.

"Okay, Chris, here's your chance to really Ac-tualize," she whispered. "You and Renee will work on Bill S. and Sally. Treat them as you would your own spiritual children. If you do a good job this weekend, you might get a chance to go to the city and work next week."

"Gee, thanks, Edie. I really feel ready to go."

"C'mon, let's do a choo-choo, Chris. Choo-choo-choo, choo-choo-choo, choo-choo-choo. Yay, yay — Pow!"

Back in the group, we engaged with the new members in "sharing." I sat down between my two guests, ready to play my assigned role. After an older member had told her life story to loosen the newcomers up, Edie called on Sally, then Bill.

Sally proceeded to tell about her family, her life in college, her hobbies and ambitions. I carefully listened as she described her rebellion against the norms of her family and her friends at school. Bearded Bill Starkey described his life as a graduate student in psychology at Harvard. He spoke about his thesis research on utopian spiritual communities and his interest in spending a weekend at Creative Community Projects. Bill explained that he planned to start a community in Michigan after his graduation, based on psychotherapeutic principles.

As Edie called on the other new guests, I carefully studied Sally's and Bill's clothes, bearing, eye contact, looking for clues as to how to appeal to them most effectively. I knew Edie was observing me carefully, and I was determined to prove to her my competence at conversion.

After Edie flattered and love-bombed a few guests, she called on me:

"Okay, let's hear from Chris. Chris has spent the past three weeks with us on the Farm. Let's hear your story, Chris."

I realized that this was my big chance. Biting my lip anxiously, I proceeded to speak. After describing my background very briefly, I smiled at Bill and Sally and said:

"I went to an Ivy League college like Bill, where I studied psychology. When I came to California, I was looking for a loving community. When I found out that Dr. Dust, the leader of this community, is a famous psychologist who incorporates psychotherapeutic principles in his work and his lectures here, I was really impressed. And when I found out how well his principles work—it's really incredible! I'm sure Sally will like it here, too. Like her, I was quite a rebel in college, searching for the ideals she has just expressed so well. I was disappointed with my professors and fellow students for the very same reasons she was. But I'm sure she'll find herself at home here, for the Family combines such intelligence and compassion. ... "

Sally's eyes lit up as I went on and on, repeating everything she wanted to hear. I interspersed my monologue with comments similar to those of the other guests, so that each person in the group could identify with me to some extent. Edie smiled, nodded for me to continue. Finally, I concluded:

"At the end of my first weekend on the Farm, I decided to stay for a while and check out the advanced lectures. I hope you'll all do the same, for I found them extremely stimulating. The people here are really helpful, and most important, they're the most loving, caring people I know. I think it is a great community, one where I'm confident I can realize my human potential. It seems that anything I want to do, I can do better in the Family, because of all the love and support given to me. This is a great place, a place for any religious people, scholars, like Bill, professionals, students like Sally, any idealistic people who want to make a better world. I invite you to come help us reach our goal, a better, more humane society."

"Yay, yay," shouted Edie, who leaned over and hugged me. Everybody patter-clapped, following Edie's example. I sported a giant grin, happy to gain the approval of Edie and the group. I am so happy here, so happy to be spreading the word to others. Such a happy heavenly child.

After sharing, the group broke up with another "choo-choo." Edie took me by the hand, led me aside from the rest of the group.

"Chris, that was great! That's real heavenly action for you! I'm so proud of you, you're really growing. You're going to become a great brother. It looks like you've reached the point where you might be able to leave for the city to Actualize this week. Keep up the good work. And remember: Every action must be done with heavenly purpose. I'll repeat it once again: Every action must be done with heavenly purpose. And the best thing you can do for a person is to convert him to the Family. Each time a person comes to training session, it's because of a divine intervention in the universe. God and all the person's ancestors have brought him here, rescued him from Satan's world. So you must do everything possible to make him stay. Promise him everything. Let him feel how bad and lonely it is out there. Let him know that he is safe in the Family, protected from harm where he can really grow. Remember to work especially closely with Sally and Bill. I put you with them because they come from backgrounds similar to yours. Can you do it?"

"Yes!"

"Are you going to do it?"

"Yes!"

"Then, let's do it!" Edie grabbed my hands and shook them in great arcs.

"Choo-choo-choo, choo-choo-choo, choo-choo-choo. Yay, yay — Pow!"

She started running to the Chicken Palace, dragging me behind her. We ran like little children, feeling the freedom of the summer breeze, giggling and laughing. Music boomed from the shack, punctuated by riotous clapping. Bodies bounced up and down, as people, high on each other, shouted:

Hey, hey! Come on in the kitchen
In the home of His heart you don't have to hide.

On and on it went, frantic singing for fifteen or twenty minutes, each spiritual parent goading his child to participate with all his might. Invest your being. Forget your cares. Love Heavenly Father. Be reborn, be reborn ... for He has finally found you.

In preparation for Dr. Dust's lecture on God and the Creation, the group sat down and chanted:

"Heaven-ly Fa-ther, we love you. Heaven-ly Fa-ther, we love you. Heaven-ly Fa-ther, we love you."

Over and over they chanted, faster and faster, louder and louder. Bill sang along with the others, hesitantly mouthing the ritual words. I knew he wanted to believe, as everyone wants to believe, in some sort of God, in divine protection, divine guidance, divine love. Didn't Reverend

Moon preach that before there can be love there must be unity? Wasn't the Family united by ritual that seemed even more meaningful than life itself? I was determined to make Bill feel that unity and that love.

Remembering how Jacob had handled me that first weekend, I set out to do the same with Bill, to establish a good "give and take," as the lectures called it. It was essential for him to trust me, to consider me his friend, as I led him through the group rituals, deliberately creating a new reality for him, the reality of the group. One of my aims was to "love-bomb" him, to appeal to his ego in every way possible. I wanted him to feel as positive about himself as possible, for he had to feel accepted enough to want to stay before we could remold him, reshape him into the heavenly child we wanted him to be. I couldn't love him for what he was, for according to the Principle he was a product of Satan's world; I loved him for what I wanted him to *become*, an obedient follower of Reverend Moon, the mysterious Messiah behind this movement.

After two hour-long lectures, I took Bill aside and asked him, "What do you think of the Farm, Bill?"

"It's really amazing. The group's sincerity and dedication are fantastic. But I have so many questions about the lectures and about the social service projects in Berkeley which nobody will talk about in any detail. And I can't get accustomed to the group life in our circles here. You know, how everything comes from or goes to Edie. Is this true in all the groups?"

"Well, yes. We feel that older members have a special relationship to God, so the elder members direct the activities and mediate the conversations."

"I find that hard to accept, Chris."

"But you get used to it. You will learn that everything works better that way. And you'll find that the older members have a great deal of wisdom."

"Maybe so, but Edie can't or won't answer all my questions."

"Don't worry. They'll all be answered in time. You have to have faith, brother. Just have faith."

I patted him on the back and hugged him.

Our group walked out to the field for the usual weekend dodge ball game. Edie was the team captain for the four groups that composed our team.

"Okay, brothers and sisters. We have to think up a name for ourselves. How about the Heavenly Hustlers?"

"How 'bout the Boonville Bombers?"

"How's that, everybody?" Edie cried.

"Great!"

"Great! Just great!"

"Great!"

"Great!"

As I said "great," I could hear the emptiness in my voice; I could feel a haunting hollowness in my head. The word echoed over and over after it spilled automatically from my lips. Over the weeks I learned that this word was an instant Family turn-on, as well as a term of obedience. I had learned to say "great" whenever somebody asked me if everything was all right, when they spoke in a tone that indicated that he or she demanded acknowledgment of the God-given authority of their orders.

I had noticed older Family members use the cue phrase in answer to their central figures even in the moments of depression, hopelessness, and despair they experienced while under heavenly subjugation. Their faces looked as rigid as mine, and their cheeks must have hurt as much as mine often did, the muscular pain of constant smiling, hour after hour, day after day.

So it would be the Boonville Bombers vs. Father's Flying Forces. Edie quickly explained the rules of the game, too quickly for the newcomers to understand, leaving them dependent on their spiritual parents, as I had been the first week. I marveled at the beauty of the system.

"Just follow me. I'll help guide you," I explained to Bill. Each team formed three lines, the front line always throwing the ball and back lines moving forward as the front-liners were knocked out of the game.

I realized by now that this was a particularly violent game, one in which a person could unleash his aggressions, his frustrations, at being controlled and manipulated. The older Family members played it extremely well, and I found myself getting better at playing it each weekend, enjoying this rare moment of individual expression. As the game progressed, Bill looked toward me, helplessly, for instructions. I told him where to stand, how to clap and chant, how to dodge the ball.

Edie took me aside. "How's Bill doing?"

"Okay so far. I've been establishing common bases and we're having good give-and-take. I think that he is beginning to look up to me."

"Good! Is he with us yet?"

"Not completely, but I'll see what I can do at lunch."

"Good going. You're quite a heavenly child, Chris." She gave me a broad smile and whispered in my ear: "Your Heavenly Father loves you!" I grinned. We did a "choo-choo-choo," and I fell back into line, into the game.

Bill was obviously enjoying the game now, happy to be part of a team. I knew that teaching teamwork, teaching that mutual interdependence was the first step on the road to indoctrination. Edie had explained that you have to consider yourself to be a part of the team before you can accept the ideology of the team. This is a most important point, for it means that group affiliation is a stronger force than ideology, which only justifies and reinforces the affiliation.

As the game progressed, I walked around Bill, encouraging him to clap and chant. The group got very, very high off this chanting. Angry faces, excited faces, joyous faces, all united under one common objective. The game ended when the last person was knocked out of the roped-off square. The team huddled momentarily and Edie shouted:

"What are you going to do?"

"Face the ball!" we shouted.

"What else?"

"Catch the ball!"

"What else?"

"Throw the ball!"

"What else?"

Bill reluctantly took my hand, and we returned to our circle, where Edie was leading a sensitivity game designed to get the group accustomed to taking orders from their leader, their center person.

"Now, I want everybody to lie down in the circle and put your feet in the center of the circle. Wiggle your toes. That's it. Now, wiggle your toes to say hello to the partners across from you. Good."

I admired the Family's genius, for I realized that this seemingly innocent exercise was, in fact, part of a complex and powerful mechanism for gaining control. I was to learn over the next few months that it worked as follows: You were cajoled to give up control to a person for five minutes, and that person structured your environment for that time. Then you gave up control for another twenty minutes, following the wave of group singing. Then you listened to lectures, giving up your critical control, since control in the discussion groups was contingent upon accepting the ideology of the lectures. You actually begin to listen to the lectures *only* to gain an awareness of what the group leaders would do to you and how they would justify it, for at that point it becomes a matter of survival.

Bill seemed to be responding well. When Edie asked for his inspiration, he replied, "I'm really impressed by the people here. I can't believe there's a community like this, smack in the center of California, a community of such loving, growing people—a real family. It's just tremendous. It's ..."

Bill was interrupted by the familiar patter-clap. An ecstatic Edie shouted, "Heavenly Father—we thank you!"

"It's just ... It's just ... well, I wish things weren't so structured," Bill muttered. "But I'm going to give it a try." Everybody clapped again. An older Family member shouted, "That's my brother!"

"Oh, thank you, thank you, Bill," Edie cried. "And Heavenly Father thanks you. About the structure: The structure is there only because we have a lot to communicate in one short weekend. But it's heavenly structure, God's structure. After a while, you won't mind it a bit."

"Okay, kids! Let's go for a dip in the brook! Roll your pants up, and let's go. Only rule is—brothers, keep your shirts on. Okay, everybody, last one in is a monkey's uncle!"

We ran into the nearby brook, splashing and screaming. I noticed how Bill's expression had changed. The worry wrinkles had disappeared, to be replaced by a rounder, more childish face. Yes, he is fully in the moment, I thought. He'd be a good heavenly child. Now, if I could only get him to stay for the week, to hear all of the Divine Principle. I *had* to convert him. It was up to me to help save his spirit man from Satan!

We all splashed in the brook, enjoying the structured, innocent fun, throwing water in each other's face. Sally spat water at me and burst out laughing. I picked her up and threw her into the water, her soft, wet hair flying in the air. Her round breasts were seductively outlined under her clinging shirt. I looked at them with delight, then felt a sudden stab of guilt as the thought of sex flashed across my mind. Clenching my fists, I stamped out Satan's temptation. I turned around quickly and faced Bob R., a weekend visitor from a conservative midwestern church who was overwhelmed with the attention he was receiving. Cupping my hands, I gathered some water and splashed it over his head, quietly announcing: "I baptize you, my child, in the name of the Father, and of the Son, and of the Holy Ghost." Bob began to cry, to cry for the salvation of his soul, to cry for God's great gift in bringing him to the Family. Humbly, quietly, he asked me, "Am I really saved?"

"Yes, brother."

"I want to stay. Can I stay?"

"Sure, I think you can stay if you just follow the rules. We'll see at the end of the weekend. You'll be a great brother, Bob."

Following the next lecture and song session, a timid but newly committed Bob shared his concerns with Edie during group:

"Perhaps I'm not spiritual enough, but everybody else seems so enthusiastic, everybody seems to get so much more out of the lecture than I do. Maybe there's something wrong with me, Edie."

I leaned over and listened to learn a lesson in spiritual wisdom from Edie as she said, "Don't worry about it, Bob. It's just that Family members are more alive, more enthusiastic, more intelligent, than other people. That's because of the amazing growth of people after they join the Family. Why, you'll see that when you're in the Family you receive the direct knowledge of God during every lecture. This is a very special place, especially blessed by God. And the Family is composed of the most righteous, most select people in the United States."

"But, Edie, I can't get over my sinfulness."

"Just trust us. We'll remake you into a new person, a real heavenly child. Just you wait."

twelve/"Good morning, Heavenly
Father."

We Family members popped out of our sleeping bags to
shake off the sleepy spirits and dutifully pulled our guests up
for their first Sunday morning of "Training Session."

As we proceeded through exercises, breakfast, singing,
Dr. Dust's first Sunday morning lecture, and another game of
dodge ball, I watched Bill closely. I was pleased to see the
playful way he took part in the childish game. I could tell he
was beginning to identify more closely with the group, and
especially with me. Meanwhile, I was fantasizing about the
miracles and prophecies that were promised to me by older
members once I had the opportunity to work in the city.

After the second lecture of the day, I casually said, "You
know, Bill, if you want to, you can stay for the theology
lectures during the week. They tell lots of things about the
nature of God and Jesus and the fulfillment of human history.

They also give you a chance to better study the tremendous principles by which we operate our community."

"I'll consider it. I'll consider it. I have another two weeks of vacation left before I start back to work. Perhaps I can get some ideas for the community I want to start."

I let the conversation go at this, although I hadn't given up on him. It sounded as if he was finally beginning to yield to Heavenly Father's way.

The group now launched into a round of Subject and Object, in order to teach the previous lecture and get greater obedience from guests. Bill clearly enjoyed it as he mirrored my every gesture.

During Edie's game, I glanced down at my right hand, now covered with slogans, orders from Edie, who personally inscribed them. My thumb was decorated with "Smash out Doubt!" Running down my palm was the slogan "Heavenly Father Loves You!" "Be Beautiful, not Resentful." "Remember Your Father." "Be Prayerful." "Humility Pays." And finally, written in large block letters across my knuckles was the favorite Family slogan: "NO MORE CONCEPTS!" A smiley face adorned my pinky.

I followed the leader, squatting and quacking in circles. We stretched toward the sun, running on our "tippy toes," as the twenty-six year old leader called it. Bill, the bearded Ivy League intellectual, giggled with delight.

The whistle blew again, calling us abruptly back to lecture. Edie placed us all in a line, left arms in front, and right arms in back. We hooked up arms, like a herd of elephants walking around the circus ring, trunks grabbing tails. Our awkward caravan trudged into the Chicken Palace this way, breaking up amid the shouts of joy and cries of laughter. The audience was keyed up now, singing together rapidly:

Gonna build a kingdom,
In this sad old land,
Gonna build a kingdom, it's at hand....

After more intense singing we sat down and Dr. Dust appeared. As he spoke, I prayed silently: Please work for Bill and Sally to stay in the Heavenly Kingdom. Thank you so much, Father. In Master's name I pray. Amen.

In the middle of Dust's lecture, Bill suddenly held the palms of his hands against his ears. In a flash, he jumped to his feet and rushed for the door. I flew out of my seat in pursuit, taking a hand command from Edie. I finally caught up with him at the brook.

"What's the matter, Bill?"

"It's—it's just too much," he screamed. "It's too intense. It's too structured. This isn't a lecture. God, it's indoctrination. Nobody answers my questions. Nobody even *questions*, except me. And the lectures. They drone on and on. I find myself getting caught up in it. And so much of it is true. It's, it's true what Dr. Dust says—that therapy only helps people become more successful in their selfishness. It's all true. And everything I believe is false. It's too intense. It's too much for one mind. And the worst part, the very worst part, is that you demand utter submission here. It's too much. But you're not going to get me, I swear it. I'm not gonna bend. I have a mission to fulfill. I have to build my community, build it on a rock. And I must be a rock. I must be the keeper of the rules, the Authority, not this Family of yours. You demand obedience. I won't bow to man or God. I won't. I won't. I refuse, goddammit!"

My muscles tensed in rage. I inhaled a deep breath and just as suddenly let it go, summoning all my psychological power. Pointing an accusing finger at Bill, I planted my feet, and spoke with frightening authority:

"You must submit! You must submit to God's will. Sure, you want to be a leader. Sure, you want to play God. Everybody wants to be God. That's the root of all sinfulness. But you must humble yourself to the Lord. You must crumble, crumble before God's majesty, for you are nothing in the eyes of God, a mere vestige of an idea. God wants you to follow our Family. It's your only hope of salvation. I'm not supposed to tell you this, but we are living in a very special age, an age where the world as we know it will be destroyed. Do you want to survive and flourish, or do you want to perish? Do you want to found a community on a few theories that overstuffed psychologists invented out of their little minds, or do you want to submit to God's will?

"You must overcome your arrogance. You must admit your mortality. You must recognize Heaven when you see it. This is Heaven, and all the rest is Hell. You must overcome that chip on your arrogant shoulder, overcome it and follow the leaders of this perfect community, this Family. And if you are obedient, if you are humble, you will rise to a position of great power. But you have a long way to go. This is the Heavenly Way, and you must submit. This is the Truth, and there can be no compromising of God's will. Salvation or be damned! It's up to you."

All the while, I was staring deeply into Bill's eyes, the way Edie had taught me. As I scolded him like a father and he started to swallow, his eyes began to tear, he sniffled, he swiped at the shoulder-length hair that fell into his face. He touched his beard, like a child, as if surprised to find this growth on his face. I stared more intensely, knowing that try as he might, he could not avoid my gaze. Taking Bill's hand, I began to squeeze, harder and harder, until I knew that he was beginning to submit. Sensing that I had almost conquered him, I switched to a new tactic.

"Bill," I said softly. "You have so much to offer to your community. You're brilliant, well educated, clever at many things. You need the love we offer so freely, and you have so much to give."

Having broken him down, I knew I must now build him up, make him completely dependent upon me for reinforcement and self-affirmation, just as the Family had done to me.

"You'll find the inner peace you seek here. And you will be able to practice your therapy, to do your research here in the Family. If you stay with us, the world is yours. You will have unlimited opportunity and freedom. Most important, we will provide the support you need to conquer your own selfish desire.

"Selflessness is what we all strive for; selflessness is the basis of all love. Here you can submit to the group will, God's will, and surrender yourself to love. Come share in this total joy, come share in this ecstasy. Come with us, stay with us, live with us, be with us. Now, come on, you are missing one of the most important lectures. Let's go."

Keeping a firm grip on Bill's hand, I led him back to the lecture. He obediently followed, shaking his head, confused, not sure anymore why he was doing anything. When we reached our seats, he sat down, folded his hands, and stared straight forward at Dr. Dust. I quickly placed a pad on his knee, put a pencil in his fingers, and placed his hand on the paper, goading him to write. He started scrawling a childish scrawl, writing "peace," "justice," "equal opportunity," "universal love," following the rhetoric of Dr. Dust, drawing arrows from word to word, circling the words.

Edie shot a glance at me, and I smiled confidently. She grinned and turned away, certain that we had rescued another heavenly child. During the singing that followed the lecture, we all wrapped our arms around each other's shoulders. Bill mouthed the words meekly as I held the songbook for him. I enthusiastically shouted at him above the din:

"Louder, Bill. Come on, let's have more spirit!" He complied, screaming the words. I could feel his body tremble and finally give in to the beat.

Eddie was pounding the drums with all his might; Nancy was leading the singing at the front of the room, as Dr. Dust quietly took leave through the back door of the Chicken Palace. Joey played his fiddle, grinning as he scraped the bow across the strings. Renee blasted away on her clarinet, waving it up and down in the air.

The audience, entranced, began swaying back and forth in rhythm like one great body. Guests closed their eyes and soaked up the joy, feelings of peace and brotherhood such as they had never experienced before.

As the groups reassembled on the lawn in small circles, I heard spiritual parents ask their charges questions like "How did you like it?" "Isn't it wonderful here?" These were followed by statements like "I'm sure you'll love it here," and "I do hope you'll stay for the week and share the principles with us." I looked at Bill with great sincerity, saying, "Trust us, stay for a week and try us. I promise you the greatest week of your life."

Edie handed out comment sheets and membership forms while the guests were still trying to overcome the emotional impact of their experience in the Chicken Palace. While the forms were being passed around the circle and filled out, Edie and Renee sang a song for the group, a slow, soothing song, the kind of song a mother would sing while rocking the cradle.

I looked over Bill's shoulder, trying to see what he was writing. He was signing the membership form! He planned to stay for the week! I winked at Edie and Edie winked back, continuing her singing. When the song had ended, Edie picked up the forms, reading them with obvious pleasure; every guest, except one, planned to stay on for the next lecture series.

The whistle blew from the Chicken Palace, so Edie called for a fast choo-choo. Linking hands together, we chanted "Choo-choo-choo, choo-choo-choo, choo-choo-choo. Yay, yay—Pow!" We shouted like screaming banshees as we ran to the Chicken Palace.

The band in the ramshackle hall was playing ecstatically once again, and Moses appeared at the stand, dressed in a pith helmet and wrapped in a blanket. The music softened and older members started chanting: "Heavenly Fa-ther, we love you, Heavenly Fa-ther, we love you, Heavenly Fa-ther, we love you," over and over, louder and louder, in three-part harmony. Moses spoke into the microphone with a comic carny voice, announcing the advent of the seven-day training session for the week. As the chanting rose, he announced the names of the new Family members, people who signed the forms. As he pronounced each name, the guests were herded into the center of the room, encircled by the Family. Eddie climbed off the stage, ran into the new crowd, told them to hold hands, and made up a cheer for them. They shouted a chant at the tops of their lungs that went something like this:

> *Heavenly Fa-ther, here we are*
> *Gathered under the Heavenly stars.*
> *The Divine Principle we want to seize,*
> *So make us in your image, please!*

The Family members bounced up and down on the floorboards, screaming and waving their arms, dancing together, hugging new members. Now the band struck up as we chanted: "Heavenly Fa-ther, we love you. Heavenly Fa-ther, we love you. Heavenly Fa-ther, we love you!" Jumping, jumping, jumping, up and down, harder and harder, as floorboards loosened and cracked, two hundred people screaming and bouncing, dancing for joy.

Everybody was high. Yes, everybody was high, and that's all that counted for the moment, this fantastic amphetamine rush. The Family, twenty-five members larger, was united, united in love and devotion. The newcomers, ensnared by love, would soon learn the price of their allegiance, the obedience they would have to pay as the price of their faith. In the coming week, as committed Family members, they would learn about indemnity and Satan, the spirit world and the Lord of the Second Coming. I knew that they would be terrorized, scared out of their socks, overwhelmed with theory, badgered, manipulated, loved, and tested. Those innocent heavenly children had no idea what they were in for, but wasn't that the price one had to pay for learning the Truth?

With a hand gesture from Moses, the frantic singing immediately stopped. The crowd dispersed with another simple command for dinner, groups lining outside for their treat—burgers and zucchini. These Sunday dinners apparently were the only times meat was served in the Family. Circles were formed once again on the lawn, and dinner was preceded by the usual long and sincere prayer led by the group leaders. People took turns singing during dinner. I relaxed after my weekend of strenuous attention to Bill and Sally.

As the people returning to the city were rolling up their sleeping bags, Edie pulled me aside.

"Chris, you're going back to the city. You've grown tremendously in four weeks. You now know your heavenly mission. The Lord be with you in Berkeley." She hugged me, then insisted on a quick choo-choo. I smiled triumphantly and hurried off to the Chicken Palace to get my things. How proud I was that I was entitled to work with the spiritual big boys in Berkeley, the suffering servants who had dedicated their lives in joyous union with God.

Edie also gave me permission to call my parents, the first time I would speak to them since my arrival on the Farm, four weekends ago. She said she felt I was strong enough to resist Satan's temptations through my parents' love, but cautioned me to pray for protection before I dialed. An older Family member was assigned to help me. After double-checking with Moses to be sure it was all right for me to call, she produced a key to unlock the pay phone outside the girls' trailer, the Farm's only link to the outside world. She prayed as I talked to the operator, shook her fists as we waited for the connection. When my mother answered, my guardian put her ear next to the receiver and listened as we talked. She coached me with her gestures as I explained to my parents that I was working for a social service group in Berkeley and with a local psychologist named Dr. Dust. When my mother asked me when I was coming home, my Family sister squeezed my hand firmly.

"I, I don't know, Mom. I'm very happy here and there's much work to be done. All I can say is that I'm doing the kind of work that will make you *very* proud of me ..." I'm saving the world, restoring you and all my ancestors from certain hell, building the Heavenly Kingdom, I thought.

"I'll keep in touch with you, Dad. No, I don't have an address or phone number. No, I don't know where I'm going to be in the next few weeks. I'm moving very soon. Where? I don't exactly know. Well, right now I'm on a ranch ... No, Mom, don't worry—please! I'm in the *best* of hands now."

My new sister smiled approvingly and pointed skyward to Heavenly Father. I imitated her and she chuckled.

I hung up the phone, satisfied that my parents were convinced that I was all right. How happy they would be when they found out that their son was a prophet, leading in the New Age. I felt sorry about deceiving them, since we had always had an honest and open relationship, but someday they would understand when they heard the Principle and the world was saved. My new sister promptly locked the telephone and hugged me before she disappeared into the trailer.

As I boarded the Elephant Bus for my trip back to the city, I broke out in goose bumps. What lay in store for me — what role would I play in the restoration of the world? Visions of universal peace and happiness, love for all, freedom from heartbreak and loneliness, floated through my mind. I drifted off to sleep to the drone of the engine, dreaming of the wonderful new life in store for me....

in master's name

thirteen/

"Chris, Chris. Get up! It's five-thirty! Get up, brother. There's much work to do."

"Five-thirty? In the morning?"

"Yes. This isn't the baby farm. We're real heavenly workers in Berkeley. We have a whole world to convert."

"Uh, thanks, Keith. But I could really use another hour of sleep. I was up until twelve-thirty studying the *Divine Principle*."

"Studying the *Principle*? Well, *I* stayed in the prayer room, praying until two A.M. You're lazy, that's all. That's your fallen nature. Work to overcome it and soon you'll find it easy to Ac-tualize on four hours of sleep. As for the *Principle*, there'll be plenty of time to study it if you need to. But if you work hard in the Family, your Heavenly Father will give you the Principle as revelation when you work. Now, hurry up and get dressed. We have group prayer in the prayer room at six. It's up on the fourth floor. C'mon. Get moving, brother!"

I shook my head, looked around the bare room, and realized that I was back in the Berkeley mansion I had entered that Friday night four weeks ago. I could barely recall stumbling out of the bus and up the stairs last night with my new brothers.

Keith took my hands and pulled me out of my warm sleeping bag. He led me to the shower, where twenty brothers were busily scrubbing up under five shower nozzles. In a flash they had dried off, jumped into their clothes, adjusted their skinny ties and secondhand suits. It would be five months until I would be given such a privilege, a pinstripe from the Salvation Army with a seven-dollar price tag.

Keith splashed me with cold water, soaped my back and legs while I stood helplessly under the frigid torrent. Then he pushed me out of the shower, grabbed my towel, and started to dry my hair.

"Get goin', brother! Be in the prayer room in three minutes!" I shaved rapidly, cutting my chin. The blood dripped down my neck, staining my white collar. I hurriedly blotted the nick with a piece of tissue and ran into our communal bedroom, where eight brothers were zipping up their zippers and stepping into well-worn shoes. I rolled up my sleeping bag and followed them to the fourth floor.

As I approached the prayer room door, I heard loud chanting. Brothers stood on one side of the room, sisters on the other, swaying back and forth in slow rhythm.

I joined the circle and started chanting in unison. We sang a few familiar Family songs to work ourselves into the proper "holy" mood. Then, under Christine's direction, the group separated into men and women, the men facing east and the women standing behind them. On the floor, facing the brothers, stood a little picture surrounded by a simple gold frame. I squinted, unable to make out what the picture represented. Suddenly, everyone around me fell to their knees in unison, bowed to the picture, and proclaimed in one voice something like this:

"Father, dearest Father. O Master of the spirit world, our new Messiah, the Creator and giver of true life, our key to the Heavenly Kingdom. Father, Heavenly Father, bless you and keep you well, to fulfill your mission on earth, to subjugate Satan's world and bring forth the reign of the Messiah for ten thousand years. Father, we pledge our lives to you, our hearts, our souls!"

With this, the forty brothers and sisters placed the backs of their right hands on their foreheads, their left hands over their right, so that their left palms faced the gold-framed picture.

"Heavenly children! Bow!" Christine shouted, and in unison all forty bodies touched their hands and heads to the carpeted floor, bowing to the small picture, their eyes shut. I instinctively imitated the others. After a moment, everybody lifted their heads, rose to their knees, and bowed twice more. As I bowed the third time, I strained to get a good look at the photo. It portrayed a plump, balding Korean man with a piercing stare. His corpulent body, encased in a double-knit suit, was topped by a round, moonlike face. He was holding hands with a short Korean woman, who looked about twenty years younger than he. Dressed in a beautiful Oriental costume, her sad eyes radiated compliance and submission. Both figures were wearing white gloves, symbols of purity, I presumed. This must be the mysterious Reverend Moon and his wife, the people that Family members spoke about with such secrecy on the farm.

Christine addressed the brothers and sisters, who had begun to weep silently:

"Father assures that no matter how sinful, no matter how worthless we are, he loves us and accepts us. He has taken on the burden of saving the world, and we must work to humbly serve him. Everybody must now pray. Pray first for our True Father and True Mother, the centers of the Cosmos. Then pray for your mission. Pray for your brothers and sisters. Finally, pray for yourselves, pray tearfully and repentfully. Heavenly Father will answer even your own selfish pleas, for he loves you so much and treasures you as a weapon against Satan's deeds. Now, pray!"

The room filled with a low moaning as the Family, their faces touching the carpet, mumbled and sobbed. As the voices grew louder, I realized that each heavenly child was repeating his personal prayer for others to hear. There seemed to be a kind of uncanny competition here between the group members, each trying to outdo the other in righteousness, volume, and emotional force. Christine, the oldest member, led them all. Sitting on her heels, she shook her fists violently, her face beet red as she cried:

"Father! Heavenly Father! Protect us from Satan, that evil serpent! Protect us from Satan! Help us build your Heavenly Kingdom before the world goes to Hell. I beg of you to work with us to help this heavenly Family spread across the face of the earth. Smash out Satan! Smash out Satan! Smash out Satan!"

She pounded the rug with all her might, then swung her fists in the air, slashing at invisible demons in rhythm to the "Smash out Satan!" cry. The veins in her neck bulged as she writhed and shouted, completely out of control, her face contorted with rage. Falling on her face, she pounded the rug again, and with a blood-curdling scream, surrendered herself to the spirit of the Master.

"Satani chigarra poo!" she shrieked. (I later learned this was a Korean invective against the infamous snake who seduced Eve in the Garden.) Beads of sweat rolled down her neck as she threw back her head, exposing the whites of her eyes.

All about me, brothers and sisters were following suit, pounding the carpet and screaming hysterically. How trivial this outburst of emotion made my baby prayers on the farm appear, my innocent pleas for plants to grow and birds to sing. I was stunned by this outbreak of hatred directed against the Devil, who was feared on the farm but never addressed in prayer. The ranting and weeping and animal screams were completely unexpected, as was the command to bow to a picture of a man I had never seen before. But I complied, and, with my eyes closed, I mumbled to myself as I listened to the fervent prayers surrounding me, trying desperately to be heavenly like the others. I opened my eyes and glanced over at Warren, another new Family member. His face mirrored my own bewilderment. As our eyes met, we both looked away and feigned prayer.

Suddenly, the room grew quiet. I looked up and saw that Christine's face was calm and smooth, radiating a look of angelic beauty. The mood in the room had shifted to one of profound peace. Brothers and sisters smiled as the ritual singing began. After about five minutes of swaying and song, Christine began calling peoples' names by city group and naming group leaders. I was assigned to Christine's own group, which filed into her fourth-floor room.

Within a few minutes I realized that Christine had complete control over the people in her group. With her Ph.D. in behavioral psychology and a five-year reign in the Family, she seemed to know just how to manipulate people to get whatever she wanted from them. She had shiny brown eyes which protruded from their sockets, eyes sparkling with an almost mystical energy. Her forehead and cheeks were tight and shiny, and her complexion was radiant. One of the brothers had already confessed his belief to me that Reverend Moon had picked him to marry her, a wish many other Family members had apparently harbored.

Christine was initially reluctant to join the Family, according to her own testimony. Living out by the Farm in a little shack with her dog after giving up on a life of teaching psychology at Berkeley, she went to the Boonville post office one day to mail a letter. Here she saw a poster that advertised: "Pioneer City. Come see your ideals realized. Grow closer to God and Nature. 239-3665." So, alone, despondent, and with nobody to turn to for solace, she called the number, and Omma answered.

From there, Omma bribed her with little gifts, teased her, convinced her that there *is* actually hope in this wicked world. In time, Christine came to be Omma's most loyal disciple and servant, probably believing that she was like St.

Peter serving Christ. From that moment on, she had dedicated her life to converting the world to the Family, leading groups on the Farm and in Berkeley, lobbying in Washington, and making abrupt trips to the Orient while on "secret missions," as Family members called them.

I learned later that Christine had assigned me to her group because of my potential to contribute to the Family. Competing with other group leaders, she always picked the best and the brightest. We assembled in her room—a Ph.D. in microbiology, a successful financier, a stunning young woman who used her physical charms to entice visitors to come to dinner at Hearst Street, several bright college dropouts, and various others who had special talents or lucrative careers to supply for the Family. Over the course of the next few weeks, I was encouraged to love these people like my own brothers and sisters, to sacrifice and pray for them. But most important, I learned that my growth in the group was predicated upon my ability to give up my life to the ideals of the group and the goals of the older members, my spiritual guides.

We assembled in a circle inside the little room. Two members served the breakfast—a cup of hot chocolate and a glass of orange juice. Christine explained to me that here in the city we must live on a liquid condition—that is, we must refuse to eat breakfast in order to show God how much we cared about Him and how much we were willing to suffer and sacrifice for Him.

Christine opened the session with another short prayer and a brief choo-choo. She introduced me to the older members, and everybody sang a chorus of "Getting to Know You," all smiles. The simplistic happy lyrics gave me a certain thrill, but I was impatient to get on with the real Family work.

Christine passed out cards from a box she had bought at a local stationery store. She told us to write to our parents, to tell them how much we loved them and missed them and how happy we were. We had five minutes to finish the notes....

I searched desperately for an appropriate card among the varieties of clowns and puppy dogs. None of them

154

seemed right, since my last letter to my parents had included a short explanation about the relationship between relativity physics and developmental phenomenology.

Christine spontaneously opened up a black notebook with the title "Master Speaks," a name I recognized well. As she read, I gazed around the room. The front wall was decorated with various foreign emblems. On the nearby table and chest of drawers I noticed pictures of the Messiah with his arms around Christine, the Messiah biting into a burger at McDonald's, Master praying at a large rally in Seoul, chopping the air with a karate shot directed against Satan. Christine read Reverend Moon's writing with tremendous conviction. She told us about the nature of the spirit world, the realm of angels and demons, our ancestors, and the nature of life in the hereafter. She spoke of how all the great men in history were now working for Father, including Jesus — who, according to one leader, has cut his hair and beard and now walks around in a suit just like the other brothers in the Family.

Christine told us about the Holy Ground, 144 places in America which Father had blessed and claimed as Heavenly soil, the first places where the Heavenly Kingdom had been established on earth.

We were informed that in our time of greatest doubt we must go to the Holy Ground, fall on our faces and remain there until our doubts had disappeared; by doing this, Christine guaranteed that we would not get possessed.

Christine shut the large black notebook abruptly and announced that soon new Family members would get to visit the Oakland Holy Grounds which Father consecrated a few years ago. She promised us that there we would *really* grow close to God and know that the Kingdom is coming.

"Isn't that great?" she shouted.

"Great!" we shouted.

Everybody followed Christine as she clapped her hands loudly, building up to a frantic rhythm. Clap-clap-clap-clap, clap-clap-clap-clap-clap, clap-clap-clap-clap, clap-clap-clap-clap. Suddenly, Freddie pulled out a harmonica, playing a four-note sequence repeatedly. The clapping increased in intensity and several people closed their eyes, losing themselves in the simple rhythm the same way they had during Joe Cocker or Grateful Dead concerts, while stoned or tripping in the days when the world was their private domain, a reservoir from which to experience a few occasional moments of intense joy. They no longer needed the light show or the blazing of electric guitars, the amazing rush of cocaine or the free experience of acid space. No, these were simply freaks, as we all were freaks, in some sense, seeking simple highs, the highs of a gesture, of a refrain. Here in this stuffy room they were experiencing a new kind of high, based on the Master's words, grateful for this precious chance to get high once again.

Suddenly, Christine stopped clapping and the others stopped with her.

"Children, are we going to do it?" she cried. "Are you going to build the Heavenly Kingdom?"

"Yes!" we shouted in chorus.

"Then, how do you feel?"

"Great!"

"Will you become obedient followers, *real pioneers*?"

"Yes!" we chanted.

"Then, let's do it! Here are your assignments for today. Keith, Chris, Grayson, Maria, you'll go flower-selling. Wilson, Susan, Steve, Freddie, Anne, and Carol, you'll witness on the Berkeley campus. Remember, you're to seek only the best, only the most idealistic, only the most qualified, candidates for the Heavenly Kingdom. And flower-sellers, remember that every flower sold for the Messiah is a chance to enable the buyer to come to the Heavenly Kingdom sooner. You're not just selling blessings. You're selling tickets to Heaven!" With the words "tickets to Heaven!" her voice rose dramatically.

The session ended with a few children's songs about flowers and happiness, followed by some impassioned prayers by Christine, to which the group responded with wailing and loud sobs.

I followed Keith down the steps, through the kitchen, then out to one of the flower vans of the Family's fleet, a white Chevy van which pulled up to the house with enough flowers in the back to glorify any funeral. Within minutes, the eight of us were riding along, singing more children's songs as we sped through the streets of Berkeley. Each time I tried to look out the window, one of the older brothers would snap his fingers in my face. "Hey, Chris, stop *spacing out*! We have a mission to fulfill!"

After a forty-five-minute drive, Carl, our team leader, finally pulled up at the edge of a small city somewhere in the Bay Area. He ordered me to go flower-selling with Keith, who promised to show me all the tricks.

"Keith's our best salesman. He'll show you the real Heavenly Way!"

After a gigantic, enthusiastic group choo-choo, we shot out of the van clutching armfuls of fresh roses, still wet and icy-cold. Keith directed me to a space behind a nearby Shell station, where we knelt for a final prayer. We choo-chooed once more, then turned and ran into the station, smiles on our well-scrubbed faces.

"Buy some flowers for a Christian youth group?"

"What?"

"Some flowers. Look, fresh-cut roses."

Keith waved a bouquet in the face of the sleepy attendant.

"What would I want flowers for?"

"Don't you have a wife?"

"Nope, just a dog and a cat, and they don't need no flowers around."

"Well, well," Keith paused. "Would you like to help some needy children? Have you thought how God loves little children..."

"How much?"

"Only a three-dollar donation for half a dozen, five dollars for a dozen."

"Well, if it's really for needy children ... Ok, I'll buy a half-dozen."

"What about all the programs that Christians run for these children? Think about it, think about all of these poor, deprived children, think about..."

"Okay, goddammit, give me a dozen. Here's five dollars. Now, go get lost, you, you do-gooders."

Keith paused to wrap a bundle, greedily fingered the bill, and stuffed it into his pocket. Within my mind a grateful voice whispered: Thank you so much, Heavenly Father, for letting this man follow the road to your Kingdom. Thank you, Father, bless him, Father. In Master's name I pray. Amen.

We hurried out of the office, leaving the dazed attendant holding a bunch of flowers in his grease-stained hands. Keith turned to me as we trotted along, smiling triumphantly.

"See how I did it?"

"Yes. Very clever. But does the Family really work with needy children?"

"Did I say we did?"

"No, but you implied it."

"Did I *say* we did?"

"Well, you gave him that impression."

"Well, what's wrong with that? He certainly wouldn't believe me if I told him the truth, if I told him that the Messiah walks the earth and that buying these flowers is an invitation to Heaven."

"But that's still misleading them. And you know that we aren't even a Christian group. We don't believe in the divinity of Jesus."

"So what? It's for his soul and the glory of Heaven. Look, wouldn't you deceive a little to save the man's soul? It's called Heavenly Deception. Not Satan's deception, mind you. It's turning Satan against himself, using Satan's money to build the Heavenly Kingdom."

"I, I just can't buy that. I can't do it."

"Look, child, do you want to grow to perfection or not? Do you want to save the world and serve the Messiah or not? If you do, then you must play by the rules. Now, you must repent to Father and Heavenly Father. Go ahead. Go over there and pray."

I obeyed reluctantly, crouching down in nearby bushes. Squeezing my hands together until they were mottled with white and red blotches, I closed my eyes and begged for forgiveness.

Keith had sold several bunches by the time I had finished my tearful pleas. Stuffing his money in his pocket, he set off at full speed through a supermarket parking lot. By the time I caught up with him, he had ducked into a TV repair shop. I stood outside, catching my breath. In a few minutes, Keith came to the door.

"Where were you, child?" he asked sharply. "Don't you know the Flower Team Motto: Chant-pray-run? You're supposed to keep up with me. And why aren't you inside the store chanting for me? Ya know, we need the backing of spirit world if we're ever gonna conquer this world. Ya know, we need to summon up all the ancestors and get them together behind the customers to influence them to buy flowers. I'll bet you weren't even praying out there. You better get things straight if you ever want to become a heavenly child."

I began to cry, feeling helpless, lost, rejected. I desperately needed somebody to cling to. After all, I was so new to the Heavenly Way. My new identity was crumbling under Keith's attack, and I had worked *so* hard to deny my pregroup history, my old thoughts and feelings about who I was and how I should treat people. And so I felt a terrifying vacuum— a sudden dread—for I no longer had an identity.

Keith, moved by my tears, grabbed my hand firmly. Having broken me down, he would now build me up again, as I had done with Bill on the Farm.

"Look, I guess I was a little harsh. You're going to be a great brother. Now, first thing, you have to learn the rules. Just obey. Do whatever I say. Follow whatever I do. And don't question. A questioning mind is Satan's mind. You wouldn't doubt God's word, would you?"

"No..."

"Good. Then don't doubt mine. Remember, I'm in the subject position. That means that God is working through me. Don't worry, God is telling me just what to do. I can feel it. We're in good hands. Now, what's the Flower Team Motto?"

"Chant-pray-run."

"That's more like it. Now, remember, as a heavenly child you can forget your wicked past. Father says that eighty percent of your personality is fallen. We have to work together to remold you in Father's image. *In Father's Image!"*

"In Father's Image!" I chanted.

"That's right. Now, write the Flower Team Motto on your hand so that you remember it."

I pulled a leaky Bic pen from my pocket and marked up the heel of my hand with large block letters. I drew a little star next to the slogan, a way of setting it off from other recent ink tattoos embedded in my palm.

All that day we scurried in and out of little stores with our wares. Every couple of hours the white van picked up eager Moonies who stood empty-handed on street corners throughout the city. We climbed in, tried to inspire the others in the van with how Heavenly Father was helping us and guiding us. We then would drop into the prayer position as the van careened from street to street. We thanked Heavenly Father for the privilege of serving Him as we bowed in front of our little brown sacks of money. We then counted up our take, each quarter a victory for heaven, each ten-spot another ticket to the kingdom.

At noon we each received a crushed peanut-butter sandwich and an orange, a gift from God for which we felt profoundly unworthy. A few minutes later, amid much singing and shouting, Carl told Keith and me to get ready with new bunches of flowers.

"But I just started eating," I replied, attempting to wolf down my mashed sandwich with the Family's favorite drink, powdered milk in orange juice.

"Stop thinking of yourself. What's more important — eating or the Heavenly Kingdom? Put the sandwich in your pocket. You can eat it while you run. Get another bunch of roses out of the ice chest quick," the driver ordered angrily.

Keith and I hastily prepared our bunches for yet another journey into unknown parking lots, supermarkets, and office buildings. After all, we were the lone survivors in a dying satanic world, our mission to bring blessings to all and riches to the Master....

160

fourteen/ I had been flower-sell-

ing for a week now. At the end of each afternoon, we would
return to the van, exhausted. For dinner—if lucky, we would
receive a generous donation of unusable burgers someone
had begged from the McDonald's franchise down the road by
telling the manager we were poor missionaries. If we weren't
so lucky, we might dine on donated stale doughnuts and cold
pizza.

Our group was collecting over a thousand tax-free
dollars daily, all quickly and quietly deposited at local banks
by the driver.

On most of my stops I was accompanied by an older
Family member like Keith who would climb out of the van at
the same time I did, working one side of the street as I
worked the other. Each morning, we picked up our order of
roses from the San Francisco flower district. We slept in vans
at night, eight in a row, brothers at one end, sisters at another.
When Family members were on the road for several days, we

161

couldn't change clothes or shower. To even change a shirt in this crowded, smelly vehicle could tempt the sisters to fall again, might stir and excite the sexual drives now buried deep within our unconscious.

Night after night we worked until two in the morning, doing bar runs—blitzing, as we called it, coaxing drunks to buy wilted roses for the angry wives awaiting them at home. At 2:30, we would drive to a local park, praying in unison in the darkness, shouting and pounding in the back of the little white truck, punching at demons and screaming for Heavenly Father to protect Father and his mission. Ten minutes into the prayer, Father and Heavenly Father became confused to me; the reputed Messiah and his almighty consultant were mentioned interchangeably, Heavenly Father also being addressed as Father, the name we used to refer to Reverend Moon. After the grueling ritual ended, we settled down for a night's sleep, a full hour and a half, for we must soon be up for pledge service Sunday morning.

Sunday morning in Berkeley we awakened at 4:30 and sped to what the Family called the Holy Ground, as mentioned in Christine's reading, sacred ground claimed for Heavenly Father by Reverend Moon several years ago. As we pulled into an Oakland park, I spotted about twenty-five cars and white vans. We prayed openly after clutching the Holy Tree, blessed by Father himself on one of his trips to Oakland. The four hundred or so people gathered in a circle and recited the Children's Oath, a long and impassioned vow to fight Satan and win the world over for Father. After intense prayer and much shouting and screaming in this dark park, we formed another circle and sang for fifteen minutes, bouncing up and down and shaking our interlocked arms, running around the oaks, bodies flying in the air, some smashing into the trees or just collapsing on the ground from sheer exhaustion.

We soon piled into the van and headed for another town on the outskirts of the Bay Area after a few more minutes of desperate sleep. It was 6:15 A.M. and we were all terribly tired. I felt drugged. I was exhausted, my hands infected in a dozen places where rose thorns had pierced my fingers. For the past six days I had survived on burger rolls and chocolate milk, cookies and doughnut donations. Suddenly I couldn't stand it anymore. The exhaustion, the suffering, were unbearable. My feet were covered with red sores from running. My shirt clung to me, glued to my skin from layers of dried sweat. I dropped off to sleep, dreaming of vast baskets of flowers.

"Get up, child! Get up! It's exercise time!"

I began a desperate prayer, as I sprawled among the exercising bodies, to Heavenly Father, begging for forgiveness, thanking him for rescuing me from Satan's world:

"Heavenly Father, I pray for guidance in this dark hour. Help me to understand why I came this way, what is Your true nature. Give me the knowledge of the *Divine Principle*, help me to gain this understanding for all phases of my activity in this earthly life. I depend upon You and this Family of Yours. Especially inform and inspire me on these, my first days of flower-selling alone. In our Master's name I pray. Amen."

I opened my eyes to find several older Family members listening to my prayer, checking to see if it was sincere, checking to assess my "spiritual development." Annoyed to be caught eavesdropping, Carl looked away, shouting:

"Okay, everybody. No spacing out. Get centered and get back into the van. We have to clean up this town the Heavenly way today. Okay. You've got five minutes to think and pray for your goals. We'll pick up our flowers at the train station, then we'll do it!"

"Do it!" we shouted, now tucked away in the back of the van. Keith poured the chocolate milk, our breakfast, as the group slumped into more silent prayer.

"Who's got goals?" Carl cried. "Any volunteers?"

"Me! Me!" we replied like first-graders with big answers. Carl called on Keith:

"My goal for the day is to get to know Heavenly Father's heart better. I'll chant, pray, and run, and I'll work to leave everybody with a smile, no matter how negative they are toward me. I wanna inspire my brothers and sisters in the van every time I am picked up. Finally, and most important to Heavenly Father, I'm setting my material goal for today at a hundred fifty dollars!"

Everybody patter-clapped, screamed, and shouted. Carl and Keith slammed their hands against the thin metal roof with a crashing sound as the group slapped Keith on the back and shouted, "I'm *in*-spired!" and "Great—just great!"

Recharged by this mass vitality, I couldn't wait for my turn.

"Okay, Chris, let's hear your goals."

"Well, first I'll chant, pray, and run. I'll pray to Heavenly Father before each sale, and I'll chant especially for spirit world to work through me today. I'll address the spirit of each buyer directly, chanting to him, 'Buy these flowers for the Messiah.' This should summon all his ancestors to work through him to make his spirit man buy these roses for Father, Master of the spirit world. As I sell each flower, I will consider it a precious blessing from the Messiah. I promise to use Heavenly Deception to encourage people to buy these blessings no matter how my fallen mind bothers me. I'll pray to Heavenly Father to repent for my small-mindedness in not deceiving people for Heaven's good. *I will turn Satan against himself!*"

The crowd cheered as the van careened around a curve, sending heavenly children flying in a welter of arms and legs. I continued, "Last of all, my material goal for my first solo day is seventy-five dollars."

The crowd clapped, but I sensed a definite air of disappointment and disapproval. Carl said firmly:

"That's all great, but I think your material goal is small-minded. You underestimate the power of Heavenly Father, Chris. Shoot for the stars and work like mad, and Heavenly Father will help you succeed. Remember what Father tells us. If you dedicate yourself absolutely, if you think nothing of yourself or your selfish desire, if you forget everything you ever learned and concentrate on God, then not only will Heavenly Father help you, Father's spirit will be there to bless you and help you work in spirit world. Pay heed to Father. Only he understands the truth. Okay. Get your flowers together, and bring plenty of string and paper to tie and wrap the bunches. At the count of three, out you go. One, two, three!"

Two brothers ripped open the side doors of the van, and a third brother pitched me out. Stunned, standing on the sidewalk, I watched the van fly by. Keith stuck his head out the side window and shouted, "Father be with you!"

"Father be with you," I murmured. I pricked my finger on a thorn as I shuffled the two large bunches wrapped in newspapers under my arms. Red, white, yellow roses, American beauties, miniatures, babies. All imbued with the magical blessing of our Master, all specially sprinkled with Holy Salt, the same salt blessed by Reverend Moon at his own wedding—the Marriage of the Lamb, when the True Father and the True Mother of the Universe were married in 1960 to fulfill biblical prophecy.

I walked down the street and into a small alleyway, carefully placed my flowers on the ground, and said a special prayer. Then I gathered my flowers together, arranging them so that the most beautiful blooms stood out clearly and the dead ones were carefully hidden, as I had been taught. Pulling myself erect, I straightened my skinny tie and raked through my hair with my fingers.

I ran past the Burger Kings, used-car lots, hardware stores, and the local A&P. I chanted away as I crossed the street, hurrying toward my destination, an industrial park. "Big Boy Metal Works." Below the sign posted a warning: "Positively No Soliciting!" That meant I'd have to play smart. "Become a Heavenly Guerrilla. We're carrying our war to the streets," as Keith had told me so many times. He described these places as "kick-outs." You had to use your Heavenly Determination to get past the managers and guards. You had to sell as much as possible before the police caught you. There was big money to be made in the factories, according to Family veterans.

Could I do it? If I only had faith...

I sped over to the corner of the building, squatted beside a bush, and said another brief prayer. As I knelt there, a wind whisked by—a cool, gentle wind, confirming that the spirit world was ready and able to guide me. I felt comforted by the Holy Spirit, which according to Reverend Moon's doctrine is the proper bride of Jesus given to Jesus in spirit world because he failed to marry on earth.

I stood up, grabbed my roses, ran over to a back door marked: "Positively No Admittance!" As I opened the door, I was overwhelmed by the whirring of metal cutting metal, huge buzz saws slicing through sheets of glinting steel. At the end of the block-long factory I noticed a huge bucket, forty feet high, spilling and splashing hot orange iron into waiting molds. Hard-hatted men scurried on ramps above me, their faces black with grease, the overwhelming smell of stale sweat radiating from their bodies. The noise was deafening.

I sidled across the wall, escaping the notice of the busy men. I felt a lump in my throat, for I was frightened of being caught by an angry guard or falling in the path of a crane or truck. I felt my shirt grow wet at the armpits, my knees began to shake. "Come on, Chris," I murmured. "Remember what Father said. In five years this must all belong to Heaven. Only you can do it, Chris. God has personally chosen you to fulfill this mission. Will you fail God, will you fail all these people, just because you're weak-willed?

"I'll do it! By God, I'll do it!"

I headed for the back of the huge structure where a group of welders were busy at their craft. Squinty eyes peering intently through the windows in their scorched face masks. Sneaking up to the first welder, I tapped him on the back. He whipped around and shut off his torch.

"Wah?"

"I said, Would you like to buy some flowers?"

Lifting his mask, he looked at me, bewildered. "Are you serious?"

"Sure I'm serious. I have some nice roses for you. Take them to your girl friend."

"Whatcha doing here, kid? If the boss sees you, he'll kill you." The old man's bright brown eyes sparkled above his hooked Sicilian nose.

"I'm from a worldwide Christian organization. We're promoting peace in foreign lands, helping immigrants in the United States. Will you buy some roses as a donation?"

"Listen, kid. You shouldn't be in here, especially without a hat or goggles."

A buzz saw suddenly started up behind me with a dull whir and a roar, shooting metal filings in the air. I winced at a sudden sharp pain, and stabbed at my eyes. I must have caught some of the metal slivers. But I must transcend it, for Heavenly Father was calling me for this more important mission. It didn't matter if we were injured, even dead, for Heavenly Father would give us an eternal spirit body. I had been reassured of this so many times when I had complained about my safety or health to Family members.

"Help us out, please, sir. We're doing some great work for the blind, the helpless, the indigent."

"Kid, you better get out of there now. Here comes the guard."

I blinked my eyes in pain and ducked behind the huge steel buzz saw. The guard approached the welder.

"Okay, where's the little fucker? I caught you talking to him. These damned religious fanatics keep sneaking in here, selling flowers and disturbing you guys. Where is he?"

The welder pointed to the buzz saw. Shaking with fear, I chanted for spirit world to help me, my eyes moving from a steel-tipped foot to a pair of work pants, a shirt overflowing out of the pants, a badge.

The guard, a burly man with the odor of beer on his breath, grabbed me by the scruff of the neck. I prayed to Heavenly Father that it would all be over soon.

"Now, you get the hell out of here and be glad I haven't called the cops. If I catch you in here once more, they'll have to cart you away in an ambulance. I mean it! Let's march."

He roughly escorted me to the nearest exit and pushed me out the door. I blinked my stinging eyes and took a deep breath. Determined, I sneaked around to the back of the factory. I wasn't going to let this kick-out get the best of me. Spirit world, let's go!

I opened the door and found myself in a brightly lit office filled with engineers and draftsmen. I approached a middle-aged man who was bent over a large drawing of a steel bridge.

"Hi."

He wore a cross around his neck. That was a good sign. The spirit world could probably work through him, and I could pretend I was working for Christians, as Keith had taught me.

"Hello. What can I do for you?"

"I'm selling flowers for a Christian youth organization in the Bay Area. Would you care to buy a dozen? Only five dollars a dozen."

A door suddenly flew open. The guard burst through, a look of rage on his beefy face. As I dashed for the exit, his hand gripped my arm like a clamp.

"Okay, kid. This is it!" The guard pushed me out the door as he continued to squeeze my arm. Outside now, I desperately fought to get free. After a short scuffle, I finally slipped away, flying down the street as fast as my aching legs could carry me.

Running away, faster and faster, I suddenly turned a convenient corner and dashed into a little ice cream store. As I slid into a seat at the counter, frantically trying to catch my breath, I prayed that the guard wouldn't find me.

"Uh, do you have some ... cookies? Cookies and milk, please."

I checked my wallet, found a dollar of my own money, my last dollar from my trip West that I had been saving for emergencies. The waitress disappeared, then quickly returned with a giant sugar cookie on an aqua plate and a glass of cold milk. I nervously downed the milk and chewed up the cookie. One. Two. Three. Down it went. I slumped back in my chair, crying and shuddering.

"What's the matter, boy?" the waitress asked. I didn't bother to reply. I wallowed in self-pity, I blamed myself for my sinfulness, worried that Satan almost claimed my body. I suddenly felt nauseated. Why, I just ate Satan's food! It was always customary in the Family to consecrate Satan's food, the food of the world outside the Family, by blowing on it three times. And I had forgotten. Oh, how sinful I was! Satan would surely accuse me. And I had spent my last dollar for my own sinful self-centered desire. Oh, I'm so sorry, my Heavenly Father.

I felt more sick, violently ill. I hurriedly slipped down from my stool and headed for the room marked "Men" at the back of the shop. Opening the door, I lifted the seat of the commode and leaned over the bowl, splashing orange and yellow chunks on my shirt and pants. I heaved again and again, expelling Satan's food, retasting the cookie and this morning's chocolate milk.

Finally I closed the cover, flushed the commode, wiped my mouth, washed my hands. As I staggered toward the door, I suddenly felt that I couldn't go on anymore. This was the end. This all seemed so insane. I was utterly lost. I felt like a lost little child, a cosmic child, confused by my own concepts, with nowhere to turn. What could I do? Should I run outside and join my van, now waiting for me three blocks away? No, I musn't put myself back in their hands. They were all crazy, too.

Maybe I could call my parents. Perhaps they could help me ... But how could I possibly explain the trouble I was in? How could I explain this whole new world of mine, the farm, True Parents, the *Divine Principle*? How could I justify the lies I had told them? How could they possibly accept what I had become?

But I had to give it a try. It was my only chance to get out. I managed to get to the phone, deposited a dime I found deep in one pocket, dialed, asked the operator to place a collect call. Surely they'd understand.

One ring, two rings ... seven, eight rings.

I'm sorry, sir, but your party does not answer."

"Oh my God," I groaned. "Thank you, operator."

I slowly returned the receiver to its cradle. Wearily I shuffled toward the door, rubbing my aching eyes. I stumbled outside, staggered over to a mailbox, and leaned against it for

support, waiting on the corner like a crumpled bag of trash—
devoid of thought and feeling — waiting, just waiting....

I sensed the white van creeping up behind me before I heard
the motor. Within minutes, two sets of strong arms had
pulled me inside.

"Chris, we've been waiting for you for over an hour!"
Carl shouted. "Where are your flowers? Did you sell out?"

"No, Carl, uh..."

"Don't tell me you *gave* them away! What have you been
doing all this time?" His sharp words made me feel like a
naughty child. I burst into tears. Keith immediately began
massaging my back, and Maria whispered comfortingly into
my ear: "There, there. Everything's going to be all right.
You're back in Heavenly Father's care." She filled my hands
with multicolored chocolate mints to prove that God loved
me.

"I felt really sick, so I stopped and prayed," I blubbered.
Had I lost my one chance to escape? Would they watch me
more carefully than ever now? Lord, how helpless I was.

Carl broke the silence.

"Listen, Chris. If you pray repentfully, even Heavenly
Father can forgive you. I think it's time for some inspiration.
Keith, will you read this month's "Master Speaks"?

As Keith read the words of the Master, I slumped in the
back of the van, half listening, smelling the sickly odor, a
mixture of roses and perspiration.

Keith was reading about how we must give up everything to become members of the Family. Listening to him, I
realized that everything Reverend Moon decreed was being
smoothly accomplished, unbeknownst to countless millions
of Americans. He was laying the "material foundation,"
gathering up millions of dollars, quietly buying real estate
and corporations, lobbying for his various front groups in
Washington while converting thousands of young people,
young people who were completely dedicated to correcting
the world's ills. Either this was wonderful or it was madness—divine, frightening madness.

I remembered how people in the Family joked about how crazy everybody would think they were if they only knew what Family members *actually* thought and did with their lives. Think of the words the group used: No More Concepts, You Think Too Much, Your Mind Is Fallen, Heavenly Thinking, The Heavenly Way, Follow Center, and the other slogans that saturated my brain!

I remembered what one Family member once told me about Reverend Moon's theme several years ago.

"We must become crazy for God." Yes, that's what he'd said.

Crazy for God. Father said so, so we must become crazy for God. Crazy. God. God-Crazy. And we are, I thought. We are. And soon the Victory will be won. We—are—becoming—crazy for God. We are becoming—Crazy for God. We are becoming Crazy for God. Yes—that's it. And no one will understand us—until they become crazy for God, too....

The van whipped around the corner, right rear wheels flying over the sidewalk and down, scattering heavenly children and bundles of paper bags filled with dollar bills neatly banded in hundred-dollar stacks. Soon we were traveling down a long stretch of California highway, facing a glorious sunset which shot red flames across the azure sky. Somebody shouted, "Lookit the sunset!"

"That's Heavenly Father's way of thanking us for all the good we've done today for Him," Keith exclaimed. "Thank you, Heavenly Father."

"Thank you, Heavenly Father," we echoed.

fifteen/

Five months had passed since my first fateful visit to the Farm. Summer had turned to fall, fall into early winter. I changed with the seasons and fell into line completely. I had stamped out my doubts (Stamp Out Doubts! Stamp Out Doubts!), fearing to question or think outside of the beliefs called the Divine Principle, for I felt that Satan had access to all my thoughts and would accuse me for questioning.

During these months I assumed various roles. After flower-selling for several weeks, I was transferred to a team to witness to people as Jacob had done to lure me into the group. As part of a squad assigned to stroll around the Berkeley campus, I accosted strangers, made "friends" with them, and finally invited them up to dinner with our "social action group." I frequently found this depressing, for many university students now knew our tricks. They would confront us with our dishonesty daily, causing us to retreat to nearby bushes, to squat and pray desperately in order to maintain our faith.

I had been suffering for months from several serious infections which refused to heal due to chronic exhaustion and malnutrition. When, frightened by severe coughing fits, accompanied by fever and dizziness, I requested medical attention, angry Family leaders accused me of faithlessness and urged me back to work. In spite of their insistence that I would be healed and fed by spiritual energy while continuing my tasks, I knew I needed protein to recover.

In early October I therefore requested to work with Jacob on his "secret mission"—a New York-style kosher deli run by the Family in Oakland under a front name. I realized that this was the only place a Family member could hope to get the nutrition I desperately needed. Since I had recently been told by an older member that working with my spiritual father would bring me closer to Heavenly Father, I also hoped to nourish my spirit in these new surroundings.

I began my Oakland assignment by serving a five-week apprenticeship as a sixteen-hour-a-day dishwasher. To my dismay, Jacob allowed us an occasional hot dog and little else. On my third day of work, I discovered a bucket of meat scraps in the kitchen—the ends of the pastrami slabs that would not fit into the meat cutter. I humbly asked Jacob if I could taste the refuse. When he agreed, I dug deep into the bucket, fished out some greasy knobs, and tore at them greedily.

When I began to complain of excruciating backaches after prolonged bouts hunched over the sink, Jacob talked darkly of the evil dish spirits that attacked your muscles if you didn't work hard enough. I redoubled my efforts while chanting powerful Family chants, stopping sporadically to sock a few demons or chase them away by flailing my dishrag. After proving my success at conquering evil spirits and claiming the dishroom for God, I was assigned to the main dining area. Here I dutifully sliced cheesecake or served meals from 7:00 A.M. to midnight, signing over all my token forty-hour paychecks for Jacob to cash for the Family.

I had broken off completely from "Old Life," as the Family called it. I phoned my parents every two weeks to reassure them that I cared, since Family members were told not to alienate their biological parents but to prepare them for conversion. I continued to tell my mother and father that I was working for a grass-roots social work community in Berkeley. When they asked about my future, I hedged, repeating, "I'm in good hands, now. I am in the best of hands. Don't worry about me." They once asked me offhandedly: "Are you in any way connected with any group working for Reverend Moon?" I flatly denied it, using Heavenly Deception as my ready weapon. It never occurred to me to think that my parents might be suspicious, though Reverend Moon was making quite a national ruckus in late 1975, what with his pre-Yankee Stadium splash in New York, where eager Moonies stood on street corners, stopped everybody they could, and passed out tickets to their upcoming celebration. At this time the stories of Moonies who had defected appeared in the popular press, telling various satanic lies about the group to eager audiences. Finally, there was the rash of so-called deprogrammings, where desperate parents called on professional talker Ted Patrick who kidnapped Moonies off the street and tortured them until they promised not to go back to the group. I was told he used insidious brainwashing tactics and special cruel tricks that only Satan could have inspired. Top leaders in the Family, the only ones allowed time to scan the papers, read in horror and quickly destroyed the articles before the spiritual babies could find them and read Satan's lies.

By early December, the Family was in an uproar. There had been three deprogrammings of Bay Area members within a week. Omma and Dr. Dust, crowned the True Parents of America by Reverend Moon's special blessing three years before, swiftly convened all four hundred local members for a gigantic meeting at the Hearst Street mansion to warn that Satan was stepping up his attack upon the Family. After each kidnapping there were additional secret staff meetings, and reconnaissance teams were sent around to the local airports to rescue the missing heavenly child.

As my concern for my spiritual development grew, I wanted to learn more about Omma and Oppa—Dr. Dust's name in the Family—and be as close to them as possible, since the highest leaders said that if you knew and loved them, you were seeing and being with God. I managed to piece together bits of information about them over the months:

I learned that Omma had left Korea for Japan soon after joining Moon's movement. She spent several years as a missionary there, learning how to preach the Divine Principle and bring converts into the burgeoning group. In the early seventies, Reverend Moon apparently chose her to move to Berkeley to replace a failing Korean academic who could not appeal to the clusters of searchers who had been congregating throughout California for years. It was Omma who skillfully introduced the personal touches so widely used in conversion in the Family now. Testimonies of her first dozen converts confirmed that she knew how to take immediate charge over the lives of her new children and make them completely obedient.

One day, one of her converts brought his English professor, Dr. Dust, to dinner at the spiritual house. He was soon won over by Omma's special charms, and within a number of months they were married in a special Korean wedding rite officiated by Father. Omma was the body and soul of the West Coast movement and seemed to me to have complete control over her husband, whose academic background gave him the air of respectability the movement needed. Now that the West Coast movement had its own parents, the spiritual family soon blossomed.

I had quickly become a favorite child of Dr. Dust and Omma. Admired by the group for my intellect and character, as well as my determination, I came to the attention of Dr. Dust when I was living at the Hearst Street mansion. Sensing my potential, he and Omma rushed me through the traditional training period and quickly gave me larger personal responsibility. When I started working at the deli, they met with me a number of times, which thrilled me tremendously and aroused jealousy in older members. Within a few weeks of these meetings, Dr. Dust gave me a special mission—to start a private elementary school under a front name.

"At twenty-one, you'll be the youngest principal in the United States," he promised. I eagerly began plans for the school the next day, including, of course, a children's version of the *Divine Principle....*

Every year, on January 1, the Family celebrated God's Day. As December drew to a close, Family members whispered and giggled at the expectation of dressing up like adults. Perhaps Omma would even let us sleep a few extra hours that night.

I was living full-time in Oakland now with the deli crew, a Family sister named Jennifer, and Dr. Dust's kids, whom I tutored and fathered when not working on the school project or at the deli. Since Dr. Dust and Omma were the True Parents for all us needy adults in the group, they did not have time to see their own children by Dr. Dust's previous marriage. In fact, Omma considered these kids so fallen and satanic that she showed disgust when forced to touch them.

On the eve of God's Day, I zoomed up into the parking lot at Hearst Street—as the lot filled with white vans unloading their troopers. Family members descended like flies to molasses, swarming around the entrance to the house. I saw four hundred smiles, those incessant grins that have made Moonies famous nationwide.

I opened the passenger's door of the brown beaten Volkswagen I drove and took Jennifer's hand. I had learned to love Jennifer with all my heart. We had so much affection between us that in dark, secret moments we often held hands late at night, when the children and deli crew were fast asleep. Once I even rubbed my cheek against hers and placed my arms on her hips, but I drew back as my cheek burned with love fever, a sure sign that Satan was attacking my spirit for making a common base with him in fallen lust.

After Jennifer, Dr. Dust's kids piled out of the vehicle for the pre-God's Day celebration. Tinker and Tim were six and eight years respectively. By working with them on a daily basis, it was obvious to me that they had never received the early love that kids beg for constantly, nestling against their mother's breasts, burying their tear-stained faces into a nice, warm skirt.

I followed Jennifer and the boys up the steps, where at the entrance I was greeted by Christine, who shook my hand and looked at me searchingly.

"Why, Chris! It's so good to see you! You're getting more handsome every day!" She flashed a quick smile and I flushed. I felt loved, accepted, admired.

Leaving our shoes at the door (I now knew this was an old Korean custom), we started down the hall. People were scurrying back and forth, men in their fifties suits and women in secondhand gowns, polishing the banisters and vacuuming rugs in preparation for the coming celebration. As I entered the main room, people hurried up and pumped my hand, telling me how heavenly I looked, how sophisticated I appeared, how I already looked like an older Family member. I caught up with Jennifer, who was chatting with Keith. I hadn't seen him in months. As we shook hands, he remarked, "I thought you'd be possessed by now, Chris!"

I flushed and stared down at my newly polished shoes. Keith grinned and punched me lightly on the shoulder.

"I was only teasing on account of all those questions you used to ask. I worried that Satan might attack you. But I can see that you've become a real Heavenly child. Welcome to the Family, child! You've made it into the Heavenly Kingdom."

I basked in my newly acquired status in the group, the recognition I was beginning to get from people who used to boss me around. Word about my elementary school mission was beginning to spread. I planned to include a day-care center and hoped that all those Family mothers who had abandoned their babies from satanic pre-Family marriages to their parents would finally be reunited with their loves. I secretly hoped that even these fallen children of Satan would reclaim the heavenly affection they needed for good growth. And so, tasting the power of love and respect, I stopped a leader named Molly in the hall and mentioned my scheme.

"Why, Chris, that would be wonderful. I'm just delighted. I have to confess that my little Dan has received such terrible care on the Farm that I really don't know what to do. You see, they keep all the Family children, Satan's children, in that little trailer near the barn. The kids mess up their food, mess up the floor, run like holy terrors around the crowded cabin, without any decent care or supervision. When I was up on the Farm last week, I visited my Dan, despite the Heavenly Rule that forbids contact between parent and child. He looked so sick, Chris. Nobody cares about him or any of those other children up there. Half of them need doctors, they all need schools but nobody seems concerned. I just don't understand it."

Molly shook her head in disbelief. "I opened the trailer and called in: 'Danny, Danny.' When I reached for him, he cried and shrank back with fear. I'm not even sure he remembered who I was. Oh, Chris, you've got to help me. I've wanted to talk to somebody. I've thought of taking Dan and leaving the Family. I love him so much and..."

I took her hand.

"Don't worry Molly. Perhaps Heavenly Father is testing your faith. I'll do what I can to help but remember Heavenly Father must come first, before your child or anyone from your fallen past."

Molly sighed, "Yes, I'm sure Heavenly Father is doing everything he can. I must be faithful. Thank you, Chris, for listening to my spiritual problem. Father be with you."

"Father be with you," I replied.

She squeezed my hand and gave a little bow of deference. I walked back over to Jennifer and whispered, "That heavenly child Molly is much too attached to her son. If she doesn't forget about that fallen child, Satan will take her surely. We've got to pray for her."

"Yes, Chris. I agree." I beamed at her, feeling so proud, since Molly had been one of my first subjects and Jennifer was a leader of four years' standing. I was tasting pure control, enjoying my ability to demand complete respect from others after months of being subjected to humiliation by my leaders. Now to really succeed in the Family, I realized that I had to win the respect of all the highest members, the oldest members, those who had founded the Family, the ones who enjoyed the wealth and prestige as well as the power that came with that status. This meant serving them completely, both embarrassing and impressing them with my willingness to humiliate myself. It seemed that the higher I moved in status in the group, the lower I had to bow and sweep, until there could be only complete obedience and suffocation of the will for the purpose of our Master. This morning, however, I was drunk with pride.

But my euphoria was short-lived.

"Chris!"

"Yes, Christine."

"Omma and Oppa will be arriving any minute. Go get a broom from the closet and sweep the front walk. Hurry."

I slunk over to the closet like a dog dragging its tail. Slipping on my shoes, I stepped outside and began angrily pushing dust back and forth on the pavement. Why did Christine want to humiliate me? Did she feel threatened by my new status in the group or was she ordering me around for the sheer joy of demeaning me, as I had seen her do with so many others? Why did I let her make me feel so worthless?

As I continued sweeping, a large Lincoln pulled up to the curb. Two of Omma and Oppa's guards stepped out and escorted the stately couple down the sidewalk and up the steps of the mansion.

Omma and Oppa! Omma and Oppa! My heart pounded with joy at the sight of my spiritual parents. If I could only hug her. If I could only shake his hand and feel truly accepted as one of his own heavenly sons. But no, I was too lowly, unworthy of their slightest glance.

Omma's face was framed by a fabulous fur collar. She sported two beautiful gems on her fingers, holding them out for all to see. Oppa was decked out in an expensive suit with matching shoes. I was dazzled by the image of majesty they conveyed.

They stepped up the stairs like aristocrats from some forgotten age. As they glided past me, I bowed and whispered, "Oh, Omma and Oppa, thank Heavenly Father for your goodness in guiding us." Omma turned and flashed a smile in my direction. Her eyes burned like fire, engulfing me with love. Oppa glanced over his shoulder and said softly, "Hello, Chris, and Happy God's Day to you. Father be with you."

"Father be with you," I replied worshipfully. This must be how the disciples of Jesus had felt: so crude, imperfect, unworthy, sure that their lowly presence must pain their teacher.

I hurried up the stairs and held open the front door. Omma and Oppa slipped off their shoes and donned golden satin slippers. The regal couple instantly became the center of attention, as they strolled down the hall, arm in arm. There was a sudden hush, followed by shrieks of "Oh, Omma and Oppa!" Somebody shouted, "Happy God's Day!"

As the righteous couple moved in procession past their servant children of God, brothers and sisters aclaimed the royal parents. Omma and Oppa murmured, "Happy God's Day, Happy God's Day," as they glided down the emerald rug.

At the end of the hall, Omma and Oppa entered a huge rectangular chamber decorated with white columns and gold floral trim. They were promptly led into a side hallway, their special suite. Christine called all the members into the chambers to sit on the floor, rock and sing songs to inspire themselves in preparation for the message of their spiritual parents. Fifteen, twenty minutes passed, twenty minutes of intense chanting and singing, accompanied by Christine's frail guitar.

Suddenly, Christine stopped playing and commanded a hush over the crowd. Omma and Oppa appeared at the door, decked in their virginal white vestments. Slowly, serenely, they floated over to the great center table laden with hundreds of pounds of fruits, nuts, and candy from around the world. Majestically, they settled down at Father's Table, creating an impressive tableau.

Oppa was dressed in a long white tunic which fell to his knees, worn over white pants. White slippers adorned his feet and thin white gloves sprinkled with lace sun symbols covered his stubby hands. A thin silver crown rested on his balding head. Sitting next to him was Omma, her long, silky black hair, threaded with strands of silver gray covering her back. She called out to the crowd in her broken Korean-American accent.

"You are the children of God!"

"We are the children of God!"

All shouted in one voice: "We love our Heavenly Father."

"Come now, heavenly children," Omma cried. "Let us celebrate the victory day of God. On this date fifteen years ago the Master claimed his victory over spirit world. And on this date Heavenly Father divulged the secret of the Fall of Man. Now let us prepare to pray. Girls, move to the left side of the room. Boys, you stand on the right."

Omma launched into a long, impassioned prayer to Heavenly Father to protect us from Satan, to give us power over the spirit world, to teach us to give more to each other for Heavenly Purpose. After the plea, we bowed to a giant silver-framed photograph of Reverend Moon and his wife, which stood before Father's Table. I cried and wailed with the others, feeling completely unworthy of participating in this holy celebration. I was much too sinful, of no use to mankind in my present fallen state.

We sang a few Family songs together, Omma and Oppa swaying in rhythm to the music. Suddenly, Omma stood up and shouted, "On this special day, God's Day, we have a special treat for you. You may stay up for an extra hour tonight to celebrate. Also, we will now take fifteen minutes out of your work schedule for sing-song. The cooks have a special treat for you to remind you of the goodness of Heavenly Father. Here they are! Come on in, girls!"

A fat young woman emerged from the kitchen, rolling a huge tub of chocolate ice-cream. Another sister followed, carrying a gallon pump-jar of Bosco. The crowd was ecstatic. Several brothers and sisters immediately lapsed into prayer, thanking Heavenly Father for this dreamy delight. Bill Wattly, a thirty-five-year-old accountant whistled, shrieked, yelled: "Waa Hoo!" jumped up, to help the cooks distribute great bowls of the chocolaty mess. Each bowl was received with cries of ooh and ahh. Christine stood up, picked up her guitar, and started singing "Jingle Bells." The crowd joined in, happily slurping and smacking away as they sang. I mushed my ice cream against the side of the bowl, making a child's soup out of the rich, brown mounds.

For the next fifteen minutes, four hundred brothers and sisters rocked back and forth on their buttocks, singing such Family favorites as "Put on a Happy Face," "Happy Days Are Here Again," "Zip-a-Dee-Do-Dah," and "You Are My Sunshine."

Omma and Oppa beamed at the crowd while eating their delicately prepared meal from their beautiful ceremonial china. The heavenly children basked in their approval, confident in the knowledge that God Himself was smiling at them. I knew that Omma and Oppa truly believed they were our parents, that God had sent them here to raise a worldwide family, that they were special agents of God, disciples as important as Peter and John. How honored we were to be in their holy presence.

After fifteen or twenty minutes, the heavenly children were thoroughly high from the combination of the chocolate concoction and happy chanting. Omma rose to her feet and the crowd fell silent.

"My heavenly children, we must now participate in Heavenly Ritual. As part of wonderful God's Day celebration, we will form two lines, brothers on one side, sisters on the other. We must all do Heavenly Handshake."

The audience quickly assembled in military fashion, lining up like soldiers in front of Omma and Oppa, who had positioned themselves in front of Father's Table. Following Christine's instructions, the brothers fell into rank according to their spiritual age, the number of months or years they had been in the Family. (I was told that this indicated to us how much Heavenly Father loved us, for we knew he calls to the Family first the ones he loves most.) Matthew, the first brother to join the Family, stepped up to Oppa and shook his gloved hand. Oppa looked deeply into the young man's eyes and said, "Heavenly Father loves you."

"Father be with you," Matthew responded.

Matthew then shook Omma's hand. She exclaimed in her broken English, "Heavenly Father loves you."

Staring into her chestnut eyes, he repeated, "Father be with you." He then joined the welcoming line next to Omma, and the next brother came forward to shake Oppa's hand.

The ceremony lasted for over forty-five minutes. At the end, the receiving line snaked through the hallway, down the stairs, and into the basement, where the sisters were grouped, for they were the last to be received, the shameful descendants of wicked Eve. As each new member passed through the line, he was received with "Hi, my name is . . . ," or "Hello, brother, welcome to the Heavenly Kingdom. It's great to know you! Just great." Each person gazed as deeply as possible into the other's eyes. One could gauge by the power of the gaze, the depth of the stare, just how powerful the person was, how "subjective," as the Family called it, how domineering he could be. I saw several new members stagger or shake their heads to recover from the force of a penetrating gaze. After several hundred encounters each, we were all buzzing, eyes ablaze.

As the last sister passed through the welcoming line, Omma clapped her hands. The line immediately broke up, brothers and sisters swarming like bees through the house to form their original phalanx. At a nudge by Omma, Oppa exclaimed:

"We have a special surprise for you. We have just received word that Father has flown into Berkeley to visit us on this most special occasion. For the next few hours you must fall into your work crews. Center men will receive instructions from me. Now, everybody lock arms and let's have a big choo-choo!"

Four hundred voices resounded through the crowded house: "CHOO-CHOO-CHOO, CHOO-CHOO-CHOO, CHOO-CHOO-CHOO. YAY, YAY—POW!"

sixteen/

The morning of Father's arrival dawned bright and beautiful. San Francisco Bay sparkled in the distance. Mail trucks rattled through the empty Berkeley streets, picking up their bundles at the blue sidewalk boxes. We heavenly children were exhausted. After polishing doorknobs, hanging new curtains, moving Father's ornate furniture from storage into the living room, we were allowed to nap briefly, then awakened to prepare for the arrival of the Master. Despite my excitement at the chance to see Father in the flesh, I desperately hoped that some way, somehow, I could get another few minutes of sleep.

At the sound of the whistle, everyone jumped with a start. A watchful brother guarding the door popped his head into the hallway, shouting, "Father's here! Father's here!"

Omma and Oppa descended from their private bedroom to welcome the glorious Messiah and his retinue. Christine blew the whistle again, and brothers and sisters assembled in rows and columns. Christine started the chant to summon the spirit world. "Glory to Heaven, Peace on Earth, Glory to Heaven, Peace on Earth, Glory to Heaven, Peace on Earth..." The bells in the nearby church tolled six o'clock as two immense limousines pulled up to the entrance of the mansion. Guards in black suits jumped out of the vehicles, speedily opening back doors. Out of the first limousine stepped a short, squat Korean with sparse black strands of hair fringing his smooth, round head. The guards immediately bowed and shut the doors. Several other distinguished-looking Orientals climbed out of the remaining cars.

The man we called our Father marched briskly up the stairs and through the doorway. He rushed down the hall, passing me and the others in line, and burst into the living room as though he owned the entire world. Thirty paces behind him followed his sad-eyed fragile wife. They sat down together at Father's Table, magnificently laid with silver goblets, Lenox china, and the finest Waterford crystal, which gleamed in the morning sunlight.

The atmosphere was electric. I had never seen Father before, but he seemed much smaller and much harder-looking than I had ever imagined. I marveled at my great fortune. Here I was living at the most crucial moment in history, in the center of the richest, most progressive nation on earth, face to face with the most important man in the history of the universe. As the Family stood at attention, the Messiah sipped silently from his glass, surveying the crowd with indifference.

The room was circled by guards, huge Asians and Europeans in black suits, well drilled in the martial arts. The doors were locked, the windows tightly shut. Christine shouted, "Bow!" and we complied, all four hundred of us simultaneously inclining from the waist for Father. Christine shouted, "Down!" and we immediately sank to our knees, dropping our heads three times for the Master.

The Messiah continued to sip his drink as his faithful translator, Colonel Peck, a former Korean military leader who carried himself like a polished diplomat, stepped up to the microphone. He addressed us softly, saying something like this:

"How fortunate you are that Father has agreed to talk to you today. He wants to tell you he loves you in spite of your fallen nature and even Heavenly Father loves you because you work so hard for him. And now, Master speaks!"

Reverend Moon pushed back his chair and stepped up to the microphone beside his translator. The crowd, sitting in rows, applauded wildly, and everybody rose on their knees to get a better look at their Messiah. The chunky Korean began to scream at the top of his lungs, pausing intermittently for his translator to interpret. I looked on in wonder as Father danced across the room, ranting and yelling. Colonel Peck spoke, and I remember hearing:

"Father asks you what you expect to see in the Messiah. Father wants you to know that he is human, too. Father wants you to know that even *he* goes to the bathroom. Have you ever thought that the Messiah is *that* human?"

The crowd cheered and laughed wildly.

"Father says you can be sure that he's the Messiah because God made him the handsomest man on earth." The children chuckled, Moon beamed....

"Now, Father is very tired. He has been praying all night for you, so he has decided he will not speak to you today. You don't mind, do you?" Peck asked mischievously.

"No, no, let him speak!" we shouted in unison. "We love Father, we love Father... !"

Moon clasped his hands and shouted something in Korean, smiling at us all the while. Colonel Peck translated:

"Father loves you so much that he feels he must speak to you. He is willing to sacrifice his meal and sleep for you. God will surely judge you for this, so stay awake and listen to his word. If sleep spirits attack you, you *must* fight them off."

Colonel Peck paused, and Father continued to speak, chopping the air with violent strokes, slashing at spirits, wrestling with invisible demons, throwing out kung-fu punches. We watched him with awe and delight. He suddenly twisted around, pulled Peck's lapels, shook him, pretended to punch the colonel in the abdomen, then pushed his faithful translator away. Peck smoothed his hair and pushed at the bridge of his black-frame glasses, addressing the crowd in broken English.

"Father says that this room is filled with demons. Because his spiritual eyes are open to spirit world, he can see Jesus, Moses, Buddha, and all the sages of East and West struggling, fighting evil spirits trying to gain access to this room. Father explains that this is why he ordered the doors and windows shut. Higher spirits can penetrate windows and walls, but lower spirits cannot. Father tells us that we must keep fighting, for Satan himself is in this room, directing all the evil spirits of the universe."

Colonel Peck raised his arms and shouted, "Repeat after me: SMASH OUT SATAN! SMASH OUT SATAN! We must drive the demons away." The crowd screamed their response.

The Messiah leaped into the air, then barreled across the room, waving his arms, shouting in Korean, socking at evil spirits. Once again Colonel Peck translated the Master's words as I sat spellbound. The words went something like this:

"Tonight I have important news for you. Because of my struggles in spirit world and the success of the Unification Church, a new dimension of spirit world has opened up for us. Good spirits have won many battles against evil spirits. As a result Heavenly Father has cleared a path for more good spirits to act on the physical plane, especially in the political sphere. We call this spiritual path the Principality of Air. Now more than ever, good spirits can work through you in flower-selling and witnessing, in fact in all your spiritual work. You will be *successful*, thanks to me, Father, and of course, Heavenly Father. Of all the saints and prophets sent by God, I am the most successful."

The Messiah continued speaking, praising himself and repeating the standard gospel of the *Divine Principle*, which I had heard from Dust so often, pausing only for Colonel Peck's translation. Two hours into the lecture I began to feel dizzy, drugged. My stomach was churning and I wondered how much longer I could last. My face burned with heat, and I was suddenly drowsy. Satan must be attacking me! Sleep spirits were attacking me! I must fight them off, for they want to prevent me from hearing the Messiah. My eyes started drooping until the lids finally shut. If only I had a safety pin like other Family members ... then I could jab myself to stay awake and really show that snake, Satan!

The Messiah's face swam before me as I fought my exhaustion. Was this really happening to me? I suddenly wondered. Was this really God's special agent, my newfound spiritual father, the Lord of Creation and the center of the universe?

How could I love a man I didn't even know? I asked myself dizzily. I was constantly being told about all he had done for me, but what had that actually been? Who was this man who claimed to be the Messiah, whose mind was one with God's, this man who wanted to rule the world? Oh, my God. Of course! Satan was attacking me. He was planting evil doubts in my mind. He was destroying my faith. And look, he was attacking Keith, too!

I rapped Keith violently on the head, then hit him hard in the face to arouse him. He opened his eyes with a start and began scribbling frantically in his notebook.

"Thank you, brother," he whispered, wiping tears of shame and confusion from his eyes.

In an attempt to remain awake, I tried desperately to focus on Reverend Moon's retinue seated on a long couch near the speaker. True Mother, his wife, sat between Omma and Oppa. To their left slumped a mysterious-looking Oriental who I thought was Mr. Yamakama, a Japanese industrialist and faithful Moon disciple who lectured at the New York center. As I watched, the little man sagged forward, waking up with a start just before sliding off the couch.

As the Master crouched, leaped around the room, and chopped at the air, True Mother, hands clasped, drank in the Master's words as if for the first time, tears flowing down her fresh young cheeks. I had been told that one of her chief aims was to make babies for our Messiah, twelve in all, twelve future disciples, destined to rule the world for God after Father died.

Father continued to speak to us through Colonel Peck, warning me about Satan's attacks through history and God's victories through political warfare in Europe and the East. He spoke so rapidly that Colonel Peck couldn't keep up the pace. It was clear, all too clear to me, that Reverend Moon received his history directly from God and spirit world. It was evident that Reverend Moon knew everything, had everything covered in his basic principles of Good and Evil. Never before had I heard anyone defend the Crusades or take seriously the claims of Divine Right of the European kings and warriors.

As the Master talked on and on, Oppa shifted nervously in his seat, clearly uncomfortable in this panel of holy ones. He nodded from time to time as though he could understand the prophet based on his sparse knowledge of Korean, the Mother Tongue of the Universe. I wondered what his colleagues in the English Department would think if they could see him now. Did they know that the most important American in our history was the same man who taught remedial spelling to their struggling freshmen?

I turned my attention back to Father, as Peck translated. Father was saying something about how he was planting spies in the Soviet Union, how we are steeped in world war, and how it is time for us to build the final phase of the material foundation. I heard him unveil his world plan, frightening us by telling us that God had given him only five more years to win the war. Five more years! If America did not accept the Unification Church, if everybody did not follow Father, God would then leave America once and for all.

I sat dumbfounded. God would leave America and never return? I recalled all the hushed conversations Family members had had with me over the past six months, these prophets telling me that men would crawl like animals over the earth for a thousand years as Satan's slaves if Father didn't win. I remembered discussing with older brothers our fantasies about fighting and dying for God, my dream of climbing into a cockpit, decked out in Unification Church army uniform, waving good-bye to my sisters of the Church as I left. Tears came to my eyes as I thought about how many times I had failed God, thinking of sleep in my exhaustion, looking at food during my three-day fasts—oh, my selfishness!

As Father told of his political plans for this country, I was ashamed of how I had doubted former President Nixon as Father came to his aid during Watergate, placing ads in major newspapers for Nixon, sending hundreds of Moonies to fast on the Capitol steps for three days and march with "God Loves Nixon" signs. I thought of how we Americans had persecuted this man even after Father declared him to be God's choice for America. I thought of Father's plans to take over New York City, as an older brother had told me once, and I thought of all my tired friends who had been promised they would become senators after only a few more years of grueling flower-selling. I thought of all the political work my brothers and sisters were doing in Washington, Christine and Omma's secret missions to the Orient, lavish lunches with political power brokers in the Bay Area, rumors of Joey's plans to run for mayor of Oakland—even talk that God would appoint Dr. Dust as the next President.

And suddenly it was all so clear. God did have a plan and only Father knew it. All we had to do was follow Father— that was it—that was all! The world was turning to Father for help and all the seeds that had been planted would soon be ready. We were buying up land, we were growing, one worldwide Family, and we were already millions strong— millions strong! Father had a timetable for everything, and if we worked, if we worked just a little bit harder ... "Push us, Father," I whispered. "Push us..."

Father began to scream, blood pumping madly through his swollen cheeks. Colonel Peck shouted:

"Heavenly Father will win! Heavenly Father will win! Heavenly Father will win! Repeat it after me!"

"Heavenly Father will win! Heavenly Father will win! Heavenly Father will win!" brothers and sisters shouted in unison. Father stepped back and sat down on the sofa. As he dabbed at his shiny forehead, Colonel Peck spoke once more:

"Father is very tired. He has talked for four hours

without stopping, showing you his love and heavenly determination. But Father remembers that you love him, too, and Father will show his father's love now. He has promised to sing you a song, a heavenly song.

We screamed with joy, jumping up and down with excitement. Father gulped from a glass, then returned to the microphone, slicking back his sparse threads of hair. His fatherly smile melted my doubtful heart. He really loved me. That's why he was here; that's why he had spoken. I had been yearning for this fatherly love for so many years.

Father began a simple Korean folk tune. The audience listened breathlessly, young women swooning and sighing. We softly rocked back and forth on our knees in time to the song, our faces beaming, each of us hoping to catch Father's eye. At the end of the final verse, Father reached toward the sky with his massive hands and gave a shrill Korean yodel. He then sank back in his chair, smiling benignly at his children.

The crowd went wild, whistling, screaming, shouting, waving arms. Tears of joy streamed down our faces as we prayed to Heavenly Father in gratitude. Every heart in the room was touched with Father's love. Imagine, the Messiah serving me by singing a song just for me! How unworthy I felt of this grace, this blessing from God.

The Master rose, approached the microphone, and shouted a Korean prayer through the crackling, electric air. At the end of each phrase, he paused, and the audience screamed fervently. "Yes, Father," or "Yes, Heavenly Father." After about ten minutes of prayer, the Master fell silent. We rubbed our aching necks and looked up at him. Father turned on his heel and headed full speed toward the front door, flanked by his bodyguards and followed by his entourage.

While younger brothers and sisters stood around in the main hall, overwhelmed by the Master's performance, the older leaders ran out the door and jumped down the steps as the Korean Messiah entered his limo.

"Father, Father, Father, come back! We love you, Father," we shouted like six-year-olds saying good-bye to their traveling dad after a weekend of ice cream and baseball games, hide-and-seek and hot dogs.

The gleaming cars proceeded down Hearst Street toward the airport, as Father headed off for a secret destination to rest and recover.

We pressed our faces against the front window, crying that our Messiah had left us and hoping that God would bless him on this, the world's most important mission.

seventeen/

The dining room in the Oakland Center was quiet enough for me to work on this Saturday morning in early January. I was busily jotting down notes for the Family-owned elementary school I was planning, when Jennifer came in. She kept entering and leaving, trying to attract my attention, I presumed. We were old enough and trusted enough in the Family that we could be alone in the room and talk without suspicion by other Family members, a treat few others enjoyed.

Since she was secretly used as Omma's trusted medium, I asked her casually if she would go into a trance for me to ask the spirits for advice and thus save me a few phone calls.

She rubbed and closed her eyes. A few seconds later, she pointed to five of the twelve names of school principals I was calling for help, telling me she got "good vibes" from them.

I asked her a bit about her secret chats with her invisible friends. "Jennifer, are you always in touch with the spirits?"

"Sure. I walk through the house sometimes and see legions of spirits filling the room. All my ancestors, pioneers with hats and pans for sifting gold. And when midnight comes and we all climb the stairs to the prayer room, we are followed by rabbis, great men with long, flowing beards. They are led by Korean saints, who have a white aura about them. Christian martyrs stumble up the stairs, covered by blood from their crucifixions. There's no doubt, Chris. These are the Last Days. I see the most holy men of all the ages trying to grow through us, trying to push us before the world goes to hell.

"Mark and I ... Mark, he has spiritual senses ... well, anyway, Mark and I sit in the living room sometimes and talk to the spirits. When evil spirits come into the room, we hold hands and chant in Master's name and they go away. Then we walk around the room and create spiritual walls and spiritual webs with our fingers. You know the way I always sit on that sofa in the corner? That's because no evil spirits can penetrate my barriers. I am completely safe and so are you. So come into the living room and sit with me."

Jennifer beckoned me into the next room. She patted the seat next to her on the couch and I slid over beside her. We had been taking care of Dr. Dust's kids together for two months now. I had grown to love Jennifer—with her sparkling brown eyes which peeked over her granny glasses, her round, dimpled cheeks, her pleading smile. And I knew she loved and respected me.

Jennifer had a secret charm about her, a whimsical, elfin quality which delighted me. I believed all her exotic stories about spirit world because she was an older Family member, a five-year veteran, one of Omma's handpicked disciples. She once told me a bit about her Old Life, a rare confession from Family leaders. Separated, confused, lost in a bundle of spiritual powers she neither understood nor controlled, Jennifer was a prime target for the church. She experimented with mescalito and telepathy while attending Steve Gaskin's Monday Night Class in San Francisco back in the sixties. Her husband, Tom, couldn't stand her driven intensity, her frantic search for spiritual values, her rejection of her new Charger, her child, her comfortable suburban lifestyle. Gradually she developed the ability to read minds and hear voices. She would wake up in the middle of the night and hear women singing. When working as a dental assistant in Oakland, she would begin to hear the inner dialogue, the thoughts of the patients sitting in the chair. And as the power grew more intense, more unbearable, she could no longer distinguish her thinking from the other stray thoughts she picked up in the room. It was at the height of her spiritual distress that she met Omma while wandering through Sproul Plaza. As with her other disciples, Omma moved into Jennifer's life and took over, telling her how and when to brush her teeth, screaming at her and berating her when Jennifer left the cap off the tube.

Jennifer now quaked with fear at the thought of making any mistakes in obeying Omma's orders. She wore a string around her neck with a little red notebook attached to the end; Omma made her wear it to write down every petty chore she was assigned. Omma continually scolded and belittled her for being "bad," "small-minded," "a sinful and fallen, a wicked and crummy little child" if she neglected to serve her every need. In response, Jennifer cringed and continued scribbling madly in the notebook which she so deeply resented wearing.

As we sat in the living room, we watched as Dr. Dust's children played in front of the TV. Jennifer always let the kids watch TV in order to educate them about how spirits were working to restore the fallen world for Father. As *Ghost Chasers*, the kids' favorite show, appeared on the screen, Jennifer explained the event "according to Principle," as the Family called it:

"You see, spirit world is busy working through TV producers to accustom kids to accept the reality of ghosts and demons and afterlife in spirit world. Everybody, even these kids, are being prepared for the Last Days. All the superheroes, all the space kids on the set, why, they are all attempts by spirit world to communicate. In the Last Days, even little kids will be given spiritual powers to control the world.

"You know, these kids are very special," Jennifer continued. "They figure in God's dispensation. That is why they respond to prayer so quickly. And they got possessed just as fast. Why, these kids, they have great prophetic dreams. They predict world events, and their dreams are filled with rich religious symbols. And yours are, too, child, so watch it!"

I thought of the nights the children screamed in their sleep, especially Tim. I remembered the many times I had rubbed his back as he cowered under the covers, fearing demons would attack him if he slept, since his grades in school were not up to par and he couldn't control himself as others would like. He wove fabulous talks of spirit dreams to me, and I knew that he was a very special vessel of God.

I felt especially sorry for Tim. He was constantly asking for Oppa, and we would have to explain to him that his father was busy restoring the world. People continued to remind him that he must be perfect so Oppa could be proud of him and that one day, if he was good, he, too, would become a world leader in God's lineage. How wonderful it seemed to us that he and all of the other children in the universe would be raised in a completely new world, a world where there would be no doubt, no uncertainty, no Old World and old concepts to plague them. Theirs would be the world of pure truth, a perfect world with no evil, no pain, no suffering, a happy world of perpetual childhood filled with magic and miracles, a world where people held continuous conversations with God and enjoyed absolute knowledge about everything. We might all have to sacrifice now, including those children, but in return we would have everything we had always wanted.

Later that night, after we put the children to bed, Jennifer and I sneaked off into the little room, pretending that we had to talk over Tim's latest tantrum. Within a few minutes, we were holding hands and gazing into each other's eyes in a way forbidden in the Family. Jennifer whispered in my ear, "Heavenly Father loves you!"

I blushed.

"Heavenly Father loves *you* even more. You are his most faithful child." The young woman squeezed my hand, raised it to her holy lips, kissed it, rubbed it against her tired face. An adrenaline rush went zinging through my body. I glanced at the skin at the neckline of her dress, now flushed with excitement. We were both breathing heavily. Suddenly, overcome with excitement, fighting my impulses as best I could, I became aroused. My fallen feelings burst through the hard Moonie veneer I had fought so desperately to construct. Now I wished only to take this beautiful woman in my arms, to kiss her, to make love to her, something I had rarely thought of during seven celibate months in the cult. Family men and women occasionally exchanged glances that reminded them of old desires. Never did eyes travel down bodies, but in the direct eye contact so often used between members, one could catch a lusty glimmer once in a great while, followed by great feelings of guilt, relieved only by hours of tearful carpet-pounding in the prayer room.

I once believed as a new member that I could forget about all sexuality completely and hoped that my body would not respond until Heavenly Father wanted it to with my new bride—whom Father would choose for me after three years as a celibate member if I was righteous and passed his rigorous application procedures. For weeks at a time it seemed as if my hope would come true. Like the others, I became neuter, enjoying the freedom from sexual desire, something I never thought possible from my studies of Freud. Then somebody would come along or a dream would appear and—poof— back to fallen life.

My heart grew weak, my face pale now, as I realized the implications of this new lusty impulse for Jennifer. Satan was taking over! I squeezed my hands together, trying to fight off these lusty thoughts.

"Jennifer, you've got to help me. I don't know what to do. I'm filled with lusty thought, fallen love for you. Help me, please!"

"Chris! I feel the same nasty feelings for you. There's only one solution. Set a cold shower condition and I'll do the same. Twice a day you must stand under the freezing shower, chanting to Heavenly Father to help you. Stand for five, maybe ten minutes. Heavenly Father will forgive you for your impurity and Satan won't be able to tempt you. Repent, repent, my child!"

I dashed off to the prayer room, hurriedly arranging flowers beside Father's picture. I started chanting, over and over, I could feel sweat beading on my forehead, my armpits staining, my collar tight around my throat, chafing my neck. I rocked back and forth, back and forth, as stray thoughts invaded my mind. Could I be wrong? Maybe those were evil spirits that had led me to the group. No, No! Satan, get out! Maybe there's no such thing as evil spirits. Satan, get out! Get out, Satan! I rocked faster and faster, chanted harder and harder. I started to sing a holy song which instantly brought good spirits according to Family wisdom: "The Lord into His garden comes ..."

Maybe Reverend Moon is not the Messiah. Maybe I've wasted the last seven months of my life. No, no! That's evil! Satan is in me! Get out! Get out!

Maybe everyone around me is wrong. Maybe the newspaper is right. Maybe Reverend Moon is using me. Why did he support Nixon during Watergate? Why do all the southern conservative congressmen like his power broker ways? He wants to dominate the world. No, he wants to set up the Heavenly Kingdom on earth. No, he wants to rule the world. But God's on his side. Or is he on God's side?

Heavenly Father, save me! Give me Truth! Give me righteousness! Answer my prayers!

Who am I praying to? Why am I in such a state if there's a God guiding me? Why do some Family members starve while running desperately through parking lots while older members ride in limousines and live like kings? Why does

Omma sit at home and watch Westerns on TV while her hundreds of Berkeley children storm bars to sell dead flowers to prostitutes and drunkards? Why is Omma flown around the world on vacations when the Family won't pay the medical bills for members who have to be treated for under-nourishment and exhaustion?

Satan, get out! Satan, get out!

Maybe I'm losing my mind! Maybe all these months, dozens of times a day, when I thought I was praying to God—maybe I was,—was just talking to myself! My God, my God, I'm losing my mind. I don't believe all this madness. I don't know what to believe.

The lack of sleep, the lack of questioning, the obedience. I know how it's affected my thinking. I've noticed signs. I can't concentrate. I can't even read anything that challenges Father's words; it gives me headaches. I can't read a book or a newspaper in any depth anymore; it hurts my eyes and I fall asleep after several lines. Something's wrong. God, you have asked the ultimate sacrifice. And so I have offered my mind up on an altar to you. Now please kill the psychic pain of my lingering thoughts. Oh, God, it's tearing me apart....

I held my hands to my ears as words streamed through my mind: God is evil and evil is good. God is Satan is God is Satan. I am God. I am Satan. Help, help, God. Spirit world, rescue me, Jesus Christ, rescue me if you exist. I am love, I am love. I am hate, I am hate, I hate, I hate, I hate, I hate. God is love, God is love, God is love, God, God is...

I collapsed on the floor, rolling around on the carpet, tucking my knees into my chest. I sucked my thumb, curled up in a corner, stared at the smiling picture of Reverend Moon in the center of the room. I faded into unconscious-ness, chanting, "God is love, God is love, God is love...."

the kidnapping

eighteen/

My father appeared at the restaurant... he broke down and cried, hugging me, patting me... my chance to bring him to the Family... we sat with Jacob, I was allowed some time alone with my father ... we agreed to meet at Hearst Street to speak with Dr. Dust— thank You, Heavenly Father ... Oppa and I surrounded my father at dinner ... my father didn't touch his food ... Liz baked him his favorite cake—he smiled ... I could see that Oppa trusted him ... I sat down next to him during Entertainment, reached for his hand—he hesitated, grabbed mine ... Christine announced that my father was a special guest... she invited me to sing for the group ... Christine called my father up with me—he smiled again, nervously ... I picked out the song—we sang "The Impossible Dream" ... audience screamed, clapped, we sat down, I giggled—my father was sweating ... we ate cookies together ... Oppa, Christine, all the top disciples surrounded my father, staring him in the eyes, asking him to sign forms ... they asked him to serve on the board of the new school I was starting—I was so proud ... "I want to serve mankind," he said—Oppa was thrilled ... my father left—Oppa said it was okay for me to go to San Francisco with him tomorrow...

Jennifer and I and my father walked through Fisherman's Wharf ... sour dough bread, warm and soft ... he asked me what I thought about the Family ... "Ask Dr. Dust, he'll answer everything at lunch" ... my father pressed me ... Jennifer uneasy now ... "I have to check out of the motel before we meet Dr. Dust for lunch. I'll only be a minute" ... the Impala pulled in back of the Holiday Inn ... we stopped ... man knocked on window of car ... Jennifer locked the door ... "He wants something, open it up," I said ... "No! No! she shouted ... I unlocked the door ... man opened door—Jennifer, Jennifer! ... she screamed, kicked, pulled out a knife ... back doors flew open—omyGod, Heavenly Father, save me, save me! big men, two big men climbed in back, fat man in front ... I kicked, knocked off my father's glasses ...struggled, struggled to open door ... "Its all right, it's all right, Chris" ... I screamed, sat on car horn ... my arms pinned ... doors slammed, car flew out of lot, two vans following ... police cars, flashing lights, speeding down highway ... cold fright, chanting—futile chanting—SAVE ME, FATHER ... gotta open the door, even if I'm killed ... "Take it easy, kid" ... cars, trees, billboards whizz by ... where? where? ... one hour, two, endless highway ... small towns ... Richmond ... off the highway, car pulled into Holiday Inn ... "Up the stairs, and keep your mouth shut" ... he fumbled with the keys ... I entered ... the door slammed shut, the bolt snapped into place...

the depro-gramming

nineteen/It was Satan himself, the Enemy.

Heavenly Father, save me. Haven't I been faithful? Haven't I believed?

"Listen, Chris, we gotta have a few words together, okay?"

Gotta chant. That's it. Drown out Satan's poison. Stay centered on Father's mission.

I was face to face with the man whom we had been told God would kill, the man we cursed during nightly prayer conditions, the man we dreamed of knifing and viciously strangling. I marveled at how Satan could take on such a clever disguise ... the calm, casual voice, the soft brown eyes behind tortoiseshell glasses, the southern black accent.

That clever Snake.

"Loosen up, Chris. I just want to talk to you awhile about your involvement in the Moonies...."

I snatched up the tape recorder positioned on the night table between us and hurled it across the room. Satan shrugged.

"...You see, I've seen a lot of kids get hurt by this organization. I've been talking to your Dad about you for several months now and we feel you've gotten yourself in a mess of trouble. How long you been involved with the Moonies?"

"I'm not a Moonie!" I shouted.

"Don't give me any of that, kid. I've been following that guy Moon for a long time, watching the way he sets up front organizations and sucks people in. Here, look at this."

Satan rustled through a briefcase and handed me a long list of names: newspapers, religious organizations, corporations, political groups. I had heard that Father was running some of them with Family workers. As for the others—they were surely part of his plan for victory.

"How long have you been in the Moonies?"

I turned away. Family lectures had taught me that even talking to Satan established a common base with evil and allowed Satan to invade your mind.

"What's wrong, kid? You think I got horns or something?"

A thug in the background chuckled.

"You can sit there as long as you want with that sourpuss look on your face but I'm not going to budge. You want to stay a week? Two weeks? Two months?"

"Listen," I hissed. "Heavenly Father's going to get you for this."

Satan leaned back, pulled a Phillie out of his suit jacket pocket; he lit the green cigar and puffed away. He looked pleased.

"Good, Chris. You're responding to me. We're not going to get anywhere till you're ready to talk and listen."

"Put out that foul cigar. The smell makes me sick."

Satan ducked out the butt in the ashtray and pulled his chair closer to mine.

I shrank back in my seat.

"I've a few friends here for you, Chris. Sam, bring them in."

The lanky thug headed for the door. My heart lodged in my throat. Now it would begin: the drugging, the beating. I began chanting madly: "Heavenly Father, save me from Satan. Heavenly Father, save me from Satan."

Two young men entered. One of them looked vaguely familiar.

"You remember John, don't you, Chris? He was a Boonville baby like you. I deprogrammed him a couple of weeks ago. And Joseph here was in Scientology for a while. They've got some interesting stories to tell."

"You traitor!" I shouted, pointing at John. "How could you turn your back on God?"

"Look, Chris," John said softly. "You can believe what you want about me. I really don't care. Just listen, that's all. I know what you've been through because I've been there, too. We've both been horribly conned. It'll take time before you can see and accept that. Like it took me. Like it took Joseph. Scientologists have their own great leader, their own world plan, their own followers willing to dedicate their lives to the Cause...."

"Stop it! I won't listen, especially to that Scientology business. It has nothing to do with religion. Besides, who knows what this Ted Patrick has done to your mind? How can I trust you two. You're working for thugs, God-haters. You're all evil—evil—evil."

I closed my eyes, praying desperately for True Parents, shutting out the buzzing voices. If only Father could speak to me through spirit world and tell me how to defeat Satan...

My father's weary voice broke through my chanting.

"Please, Chris. Listen. We're your friends. We want to help...."

Looking up, I saw him walking toward me. I pushed my chair back until it banged against the wall.

"You're not my friends," I shouted. "My friends are devout, God-fearing people. You're out to destroy love, destroy God. Satan is in you!"

It was just as the Family said. Satan lurked in my parents, tempting me with their fallen love. I folded my arms and glared defiantly.

My father buried his face in his hands.

John, Joseph, and Satan droned on but I tuned them out with my prayers. It seemed as though hours were passing as I sat silently chanting. When would the Family save me?

Satan started playing tapes of former Moonies denouncing the Family on a second tape recorder but I laughed at these childish tricks. Everybody in the Family knew that being deprogrammed by Patrick made Heavenly Children possessed. Would I be rescued in time?

I glanced over at the telephone, inches beyond my grasp. One of the thugs quickly unscrewed the receiver and dropped it into his pocket.

"No chance, Chris."

Heavenly Father save me.

"Chris, Chris." Now it was John speaking. "You haven't said a word for over three hours. How much longer do you think you can keep up this childish behavior?"

I turned away.

"Listen." As John reached over and shook me, I lunged from my chair and caught him in the chest, sending him flying. Arms flailing, I ran for the door. In a flash I was suspended in the air, one thug holding me by the arms, another by the legs. I jerked my body violently. It was no use.

"Put him on the bed," Patrick snapped. "Don't try that again, Chris. We promise we won't hurt you, but we're not letting you go back to destroy yourself in that crazy group."

John brushed himself off and came over to me as I lay sprawled on the bed. He was smiling.

"At least you're reacting now, instead of sitting there like a dead fish. Let's level, Chris. I've been out of the group for a while now. Do *I* look possessed? And I could show you at least twenty other Moonies who have been deprogrammed like me, people I knew in the cult. Every one of us thanks the Lord we can think for ourselves again."

No more concepts. No more concepts. The words rattled through my brain. I must remain in tune with Father's mind and Father's will. I must reject satanic thinking. They're trying to appeal to me in my Old Life. I won't listen, I won't! I grabbed the side of the mattress and squeezed. Pain shot through my fingers and up my hand. When it became unbearable I let go and tightened my fists into balls.

Patrick pulled a chair up to the bed.

"How old are you kid?"

"Twenty-one," I mumbled.

"You're kidding. You look like a little child. All you Moonies do. It must be that stupid stuff you do in the group. You know—choo-choo-choo!"

Everyone laughed, including my father. He knew something about group life, having shown up for Family dinner at Hearst Street the night before to lure me to the kidnappers. The traitor—sharing our meal, smiling, joining me in a duet— "The Impossible Dream" — even doing the nightly choo-choo with us!

The thugs began jumping up and down with Satan shouting, "Choo-choo-choo; choo-choo-choo!"

I started laughing along with them, then suddenly caught myself. Satan was making me feel like a fool—just like I had the first time I'd choo-chooed.

"Tell me, kid. All those people with idiot grins on their faces. Why are they so happy?"

"They've found love and peace in the Family," I replied calmly.

"Were *you* happy all the time?"

"Of course." The words stuck in my throat.

"Are you happy now? You still have that stupid grin on your face."

"Sure I'm happy. I'm serving God as well as I can."

"You're a liar, Chris. It's okay to lie to me. But stop lying to yourself. I know what goes on in there. Do you like being ordered around like a servant? Giving everything up so those guys at the top can get fat and rich?"

I didn't bother to answer. I knew the sacrifice for God would be worth it once the world was restored.

"Go ahead. Keep grinning. That's right. You couldn't stop even if you wanted to. Your face feels hollow, doesn't it?"

I instinctively touched my cheek, recalling the pain of having to smile despite my misery, to "fight it out" with Satan as Edie and Christine had taught me. I remembered how I had learned to keep smiling, smiling, smiling, hiding the hurt within....

Now John moved over to the bed. "I know what it's like, Chris. You feel all empty inside. After a while in the cult, you begin to lose touch with your feelings. I know what it's like to smile when an older Family member puts you down, orders you to do some humiliating task...."

I squirmed uneasily, remembering how people had called me arrogant and faithless whenever I asserted myself or questioned my center man's orders. Give me strength, Father, I pray. The *Divine Principle*—that was it. That was the way to fight back.

Thank you, Father....

"But you don't know the *Divine Principle* and you don't know the love of God."

"The *Divine Principle*? I can quote that stupid book backward and forward, Chris. How many times have *you* read it? Have you ever finished it?"

"No, but..." I had been told by some of the older members that they had never had time to read the *Principle*.

"Do you know *anybody* in the cult who has read the whole thing? They don't give you time to read and think about it, because if you ever did, you'd see that it's all nonsense."

"You just don't understand it," I shouted, defending God's Word with new boldness.

"There's nothing in there to understand," John explained. "You're a smart kid, Chris. If they gave you the chance, you'd see that the whole thing's just a string of words."

"Did you ever check the Bible quotes, kid? They're all out of context."

I lowered my eyes, remembering how I had sneaked a pocket Bible into the john with me during my first week of flower-selling, hoping to see how well certain verses fitted in with the *Principle*. Terrified of being discovered, unable to concentrate, I had soon given up the search. Suppose I did take the *Principle* on faith? That didn't mean it was wrong.

Patrick pulled a Bible and a *Divine Principle* out of his suitcase. Satan—with the *Principle*! Attacking God's Word! Gotta be strong, gotta be...

" 'Fraid to check, kid?"

"No..."

"Then let's look at a few verses."

If I pretended to go along with their games, maybe they'd let me free. But I must keep chanting, keep centered on Heavenly Father. I leaned over the books, pretending to read. *Heavenly Father, save me now!*

"Look, Chris, you've got to stop chanting. You can't fool me, kid. All you Moonies are so damn predictable."

Satan could read my mind....

"I was just like you, Chris," John joined in. "I chanted for three days before I was willing to listen. It's all part of the plan. When you chant to yourself you can't think about what you're doing or feeling; you're blocked off from the rest of the world. Think how you drifted away while you were witnessing to people, tricking them into thinking you cared. That's what the cult calls centering on God's mind and becoming closer to Him. What a joke."

How dare he talk like that? Trying to destroy my relationship to Heavenly Father. I had chanted night and day for seven months, feeling so close to God....

"Now, if you'll stop chanting long enough for us to talk sensibly, maybe you can find out what we have to show you. You're free to argue, to ask questions. And if it turns out you're right and we're wrong, then there's no point in your being here with us and you can go. The only stipulation is that you really give us a chance."

"Fair enough," I agreed. What did I have to lose? I'd defeat them with the Truth. If the *Divine Principle* really worked, I'd be out of here in no time.

Patrick read sections from the *Divine Principle*, then read the sections in the Bible in their full context. He showed me a number of inconsistencies starting with Genesis and ending in the *Principle's* interpretation of Revelation. He rattled off sections of the Bible that contradicted what Reverend Moon said about the life of Jesus, his teaching, the nature of the Second Coming. Forty-five minutes, an hour, passed. I smiled and nodded as Patrick droned on and on, but little of it seemed to sink in. Satan is clever—even using the Bible against the *Principle*, I thought. Yet, I had to admit there seemed to be threads of truth in Patrick's argument. Furthermore, he clearly knew more about the *Principle* than I ever had.

"How about John 16:25, Chris? You know, Moon uses that to tell the world that we need a new Bible because the old one's incomplete. Remember that?"

"No, uh ... what's it say?"

Satan chuckled and opened the black book. "Okay. Jesus is talking to his disciples about the Last Days. Here it says: 'I have said this to you in figures; the hour is coming when I shall no longer speak to you in figures but tell you plainly of the Father.'"

"Right," I replied automatically. "That's why we need the *Principle*. To break the code and tell us just what Jesus meant."

"Yeah, that's what the *Principle* explains. But if you bother to look down a few lines—that is, if you ever take time to read the Bible—Jesus continues, explaining that He will return. Jesus—not a fat businessman. And then it goes on to show that Jesus *is* explaining Himself to His disciples very clearly. His disciples said: 'Ah, now you are speaking plainly, not in any figure! Now we know that you know all things, and need none to question you; by this we believe that you came from God.' Never heard anyone quote that, did you?"

"No..."

"See how Moon quotes out of context? See how his use of the Bible to prove the *Divine Principle* is wrong? See how he twists Scripture all over the place to suit his needs?"

"And how about the *Principle* view that God is two—that God is Inner and Outer?" John asked.

"What about it?"

"Well, the Jews say God is One: Yahweh. Christians say that God is Three—Father, Son, and Holy Ghost. Now Moon says he's going to unite the Jews and Christians under a higher truth. But he says God is Two. Well, is He One or Two—or Three?"

I shook my head, confused.

"Or is He all of these?"

I shrugged my shoulders.

"None of those?"

I grimaced. The room burst out laughing.

"You see, whatever you believe—Jew, Christian, Buddhist—you can't just mash them together. Moon is completely inconsistent. The whole lecture series is just an excuse, anyway. They could recite nursery rhymes and people would believe them as God's Word because of the tactics they use on you during the weekend."

"Here's another one for you," Satan added. "Let's see, Matthew 23:9, here it is. 'And call no man your father on earth for you have one Father, who is in Heaven. Neither be called masters, for you have one master, the Christ.' What do you call Moon, Chris? Father? Master?" Satan slapped the book closed and placed it on the table.

Father, save me! Fa ... I wiped the sweat from my face.

"Can't we turn up the air conditioning?"

"Getting warm?" Satan chuckled. "Sure, I'll turn it up. Joseph, tell him about your life in Scientology."

Joseph recounted Scientology stories of flying spirits and accounts of psychic experiences in that group. The Family had taught me that Scientology was Satan's tool so I tried not to listen. But from what I heard about visions and voices the leaders claimed to experience, I was startled at how closely his tales matched the mystical experiences of Family members. But they *couldn't* both be true!

I asked to be excused to go to the bathroom, desperate to be alone. Gotta save my faith, gotta hold out. Heavenly Father, don't leave me now.

I shut the door and locked it. I ripped open the shower curtain, looking desperately for a window.

"You can't get out of here, Chris, it's no use. Now, don't try going down the drain." He knew what I was thinking, that Snake!

I fell to my knees in front of the toilet bowl, and bowed my head until my forehead touched the cold green tile.

"Where are you, Heavenly Father? Haven't I been faithful enough? Is this the final test? Don't let Satan take me—please!" I screamed inwardly. "Take my life first. Take it, please—now!"

Two knocks interrupted my pleas.

"You can stop praying in there, Chris. We got some nice burgers for you. C'mon. Moon's not gonna help you—never has, never will."

How did he know I was praying? Trying to look like a good heavenly soldier, I reentered the bedroom and wiped away my tears. I was trembling.

Satan touched me on the shoulder and handed me a Big Mac and a large cup of Coke. I sank into a chair and closed my eyes to consecrate my burger. I knew they would laugh if I blew on it. In spite of myself I gobbled the greasy food down as greedily as the others. Was this what the Family called an Inquisition? No one seemed to be forcing me to accept *their* beliefs. In fact, nobody has said a word about what they believed about God. Were these people really God-haters, or simply misguided?

Patrick yawned.

"Okay, Chris, time for bed. Got to get some sleep. Tomorrow's going to be as tough as today. Now, I don't want to tell you when to eat and when to sleep—that's what the cult did. But it's midnight now..."

"Midnight?" I had lost all track of time.

"Yeah. We'll be starting again at seven. That'll probably mean you've gotten more sleep than you've had in months. Now, don't try sneaking out. Your father's going to sleep right beside you and there'll be someone guarding the door all the time. G'night."

Somebody was shaking me. Voices. Light stabbing at my eyes.

"C'mon, Chris. Time to get up."

My father was leaning over me.

"Where am I?"

"You're okay, Chris. Remember? The Holiday Inn? It's morning. We have some talking to do."

"Some what?"

"Talking, just talking," my father said softly.

I struggled to regain my bearings, to identify the black man, the lanky young man at the door, the two men about my age, the husky man with a pushbroom moustache. My father handed me a steaming cupful of strong black coffee and a paper plate with a second plate stapled on top. I realized I was starving. I tore open the cover and eagerly eyed the scrambled eggs and patch of ham covered with a glistening coating of fat.

Halfway through my meal I remembered. I had forgotten Heavenly Father. I hadn't consecrated the food. I had missed my 5:30 prayer condition.

I leaped out of bed and was stopped in my tracks by the black man.

"Not so fast, Chris. You're going nowhere, remember? We picked you up yesterday. You're not in the cult any more—you're with us. Remember? Deprogrammers?"

"Huh?" I sat back down on the bed and tried to think as snatches of prayers and songs streamed through my head. Of course, Patrick. My mind worked so slowly....

"He's just trying to make some sense out of this. His mind's not used to living without commands from his cult leaders," Patrick explained to my father. "Over the next few days he's gonna float. That's what we call it when he stops thinking and mindlessly follows cult orders. He'd even kill himself if he had the chance 'cause they believe they must die if they fail their missions. He'll be able to talk to us for a while and then suddenly his mind will go blank. He'll suddenly get that frozen zombie look on his face. You'll be able to tell instantly by his expression. That's floating. You hear me, too, Chris? I just want you to know what's going to go on inside you."

Patrick turned away and started pulling papers and books out of file boxes.

One of the young men came up and poured me some more coffee.

"Remember me, Chris? I'm John. We talked yesterday."

"Yeah—I think so."

"Come on over here by the window. We're going to show you a few things the cult won't let you see."

My mind felt blank again. As John talked on and on about the *Divine Principle* and spirit world, the chanting resumed. Over and over he asked me what I believed and why. I answered briefly, nodding at his replies, pretending to listen. My armor was strong again. Surely Heavenly Father would save me if I stalled. The chanting grew louder and louder, drowning out John's voice whenever I felt he was saying something that might be significant. Finally he threw up his arms:

"You haven't listened to one word I've said for the past three hours. I can see right through you, Chris. Don't you think I used the same tricks? Why won't you give me a chance? Why do you cling to that stuff that was pounded into your mind day after day?"

"If I find a higher standard of love and truth than I now know, I'll gladly follow it," I responded, parroting the words Dr. Dust had used when I first spoke to him six weeks after joining the Family. How often I had heard Oppa use that phrase on recent converts.

"Those stereotyped cult responses won't work either. Don't you think I imitated the patter of Family leaders when I couldn't answer questions myself?"

This time John had hit home.

"Hey, could we get some fresh air in here?" I cried.

"Not a chance," Patrick replied from across the room. "I know you'd scream bloody murder the first chance you got."

I closed my eyes.

"He's chanting again. Take a break, John. How about getting us some lunch. I'll take over here."

"C'mon, Chris, open your eyes," Patrick said softly.

I glared at the man in the chair across from mine. He looked like Satan again

"Listen, kid, how can you be conned like you are? You were taught to lie, you were taught to cheat...."

"That's not true. I'm a follower of God. I'm growing more righteous every day."

"Cut the bullshit! You lied to people on the streets, when you were selling flowers and sucking people in. You know—Heavenly Deception. You gave up your own common sense. You know the Bible says something about people who lie. You'd do anything for Moon, wouldn't you?"

Summoning all my will, I tried to stare him down. He widened his eyes and stared back.

"Wouldn't you kill for Moon? Wouldn't you? Answer me you mindless zombie!"

"Yes, I'd gladly lay down my life for Father," I shouted.

"You see that man over there?" Satan pointed to my father, slumped in a chair. "That's your father, your *real* father, the man who birthed you, and raised you and gave you everything he could."

Satan leaned forward and stared accusingly. "You'd kill your own parents for Moon, wouldn't you? You wouldn't think twice if Moon snapped his fingers."

I turned my head away.

"Wouldn't you?" His voice grew louder. "Wouldn't you?"

"I'd do anything for Heavenly Father," I murmured.

"Look at that man. He's your father. You'd kill him, admit it!"

I turned and stared at my father. His face was ashen. What had he seen in mine?

Patrick talked on for another two hours, showing me various documents from his files.

"Where does the money go, Chris? Can you name anything the Unification Church has done for anybody in the world? All the *real* religions do something for other people. But in yours, don't your Omma and Oppa live like kings while all those half-starved kids peddle on the street. You call that a religion?"

Three knocks at the door. One of the thugs opened it and John entered with bags of lunch. I looked up briefly then returned to my reading while the food was being distributed.

Patrick handed me a plate of hot roast beef.

"You thought we'd starve you, didn't you?" He smiled. "I bet they said that deprogrammers seduce you and beat you too. They even lie to their own members."

"So maybe some people in the Family *do* exaggerate, but everyone does from time to time. You can't blame that on the group."

"Chris, it's not just one or two people," John joined in. "It's systematic deception—not only to people outside the group but within the group itself. The whole point is to polarize you from the world and keep you in the group so they can work over your mind. Everything in the group is of God, everything outside is Satan. And you're scared to death to dare think outside of the Family for fear you'll abandon God or get possessed. True?"

"Well..." I fumbled.

"True," John replied.

"And as they're lying to you, they keep sending you to Training Session, stifling questions, teaching you to chant, until you stop thinking, until you're completely broken down, until you accept anything they say or do to you...."

The chanting began again....

"Fight the chanting, Chris, Fight it and try to listen," John said sharply. "Your mind is at stake."

"All that stuff—those Training Sessions—they're just to brainwash you," Patrick interjected. "They use hypnosis—you know, the eye-staring like you tried to pull on me. They use fear and guilt; they use behavior modification techniques—they use everything until you're literally their slave. It's been done before. The North Koreans and the Chinese are masters at brainwashing. *We* call it mind control."

I shifted uneasily in my chair as Patrick and John described what I had experienced on the Farm. They were attacking the very foundations of New Life, the framework of beliefs I had battled so long and so hard to understand and accept. I mustn't listen, I mustn't....

"Okay. I've been brainwashed," I blurted. "You're right. I made a terrible mistake. But now I'm deprogrammed and I don't want to go back. Can I please leave now?"

I stood up and started for the door. Patrick took me by the shoulder and pulled me back abruptly.

"Not so fast, Chris. I want you to look in the mirror. Look closely at your eyes. They look like two round tennis balls. As long as you have that zombie look, I'm not letting you go because you're still under their spell."

I walked over to the mirror above the dresser. Patrick was right, my eyes were glazed. Suddenly I flashed back to my first weekend on the Farm, the time in the brothers' bathroom when I had first noticed that look!

"That's what people in trance states look like, Chris," John joined in. "When your mind is working, when you're thinking, that look vanishes. For the last two days we have been able to tell when you've been with us and when you've been floating—falling into the mass hypnotic trance of the cult. Think about it; just think. Do those big bulging glassy eyes look normal to you?"

Suddenly the Family belief that God made his prophets' eyes glassy didn't seem to make sense. Could this indicate a higher level of consciousness? Then why was it so hard even to concentrate?

All that afternoon I scanned through books and articles on brainwashing that Patrick pulled from his briefcase. Reading was a painful process but Patrick kept encouraging me. I paged through the books rapidly, nodding, pretending to understand. I wasn't fooling myself and I sensed that I wasn't fooling Patrick either. My head pounded whenever I read anything that spoke against the Family. Nothing registered, no matter how hard I stared at the print.

As I sat squinting miserably at the pages, trying to concentrate, I felt Patrick's hand on my shoulder:

"God gave you a free mind to think, Chris. If you can't think, you can't help God or anybody. Go ahead. Read on and ask questions. We got all the time in the world. You've got to fight, Chris. You've got to fight with your mind."

The rest of the day and evening passed quickly. Sometimes I read the material simply to con that snake Satan, but in order to give a con reply to Patrick's questions I had to think about what I had read. Gradually my fear of thinking subsided and in spite of myself I became interested in what I was reading. Although little sank in, I became aware of a hunger stemming from seven months of thought deprivation. The hunger returned that had made me lug those sixty pounds of books all the way to California. I remembered the rare occasions when I had secretly opened them, fearing accusations of faithlessness from Family leaders if I was caught.

After dinner, my father read a few articles with me about Communist brainwashing and I found myself debating with him as we had at the dinner table all my early life. Exhausted, I finally pushed the articles aside, dropped back on the bed, closed my eyes. When I opened them, my father was leaning over me.

"Are you all right, Chris?"

"Thanks, I'm okay," I said quietly.

I looked into his face for the first time. The weariness, the lines, the graying at the temples, the pain ... He must have aged at least ten years in the last few months.

"You don't know how much your mother and I love you, Chris. She's behind this a hundred percent. I've been in touch with her by phone every few hours. She misses you terribly. Once this is over—and it *will* be over soon—once this is over, she wants so badly to hear your voice. Please bear with us, Chris."

I tried to picture my mother's face. I tried to remember Old Life after seven months of trying to block it out. All my old loves and hates ... my home, my family.

My father was looking at me. He was searching for something.

Nobody spoke, nobody moved.

"Chris, Chris."

I flinched. Satan was speaking.

"It's getting late. You'll have more time tomorrow. Your mind, Chris. Don't you care what happens to your mind? Before you go to sleep, you've got to think about it. You've got to think about yourself."

I mustn't listen. These words of Satan's hurt me more than anything I had heard for the past three days. I didn't know why.

Satan headed for the door with his henchmen.

I was so tired, more tired than I had been since my capture by Satan and his thugs, more tired than I had ever been in my life. I walked heavily to the double bed, stripped down to my underwear, and slipped between the sheets. My father slid in beside me and pulled the covers up to my neck. We lay there together in the big bed in the dark. Lights from passing cars danced along the backs of the curtain. I heard the soothing hum of the air-conditioner, felt my father's warmth beside me. Voices rattled in my head, Satan's voice, John's voice, my father's voice ... *my* voice.

Well, Chris, what *about* your mind? You—*I*—have one, don't I? Wasn't my mind once the most important thing in the whole world to me? Wasn't that what I had lived for all my life? Didn't I care what happened to it? And what *had* happened? Hadn't I given up everything I had ever known, thought, dreamed, imagined, become a child, a perfect child, to follow True Parents? But suppose they weren't True Parents, what if all Satan-Patrick's lies weren't lies ... what if everything I had learned about the Heavenly Kingdom, the Family, the Messiah, was some kind of crazy lie? What if...

I tried to chant. I tried to push away the evil thought buzzing in my ears. But the chanting didn't work. The demons wouldn't leave me. *They were in me.* I tried to block them, I tried to imagine True Parents. Omma and Oppa, help me. Please...

But the voices persisted, two minds struggling, Old and New. One that looked and thought and examined, the other reciting Family revelation. Both of them *mine.* No bridge between them. No moving back. Got to go *on.* Gotta be a new self, a third self, the best of the two minds, yet something far greater. Can't be afraid. Must kill the demons. I can do it. I have to. God how I long for the freedom to think again ... Gonna make it, gonna...

The hum of the air-conditioner faded away as I drifted into heavy, dreamless sleep. I could feel myself rolling ... rolling ... as if on a great ocean liner slowly rocking its way home in the evening sea.

In the quiet of early morning I opened my eyes and saw my father beside me.

He stirred, stretched, opened his eyes. He turned to me.

"Chris," he said.

"Dad..."

The odor of black coffee penetrated my consciousness, awakening me from deep peaceful sleep. Looking around the room, I saw the members of my deprogramming team packing their bags. I rejoiced at the thought of walking out

226

into the sunlight and fresh air. Although I was uncertain as to where I was going, I looked forward to doing what I had hoped to do ever since the first week on the Farm—to fully examine the Family practices and ideology. I looked forward to making my own decisions, to doing what I had always treasured most—questioning and thinking about life situations, especially my own. I knew now that my thinking ability in the group had deteriorated rapidly—that I had finally, in despair, offered my mind up onto the altar of God. Patrick and John warned me that as I gained insight into my life in the Moonies, I would realize what kind of damage the cult's childhood states and subservient roles, the chanting, the lack of intellectual stimulation, and other factors had done to me. They warned me that it might be months before I could function as effectively in the world as I had before I met the group. They told me that I would have to be patient with myself and work to restore my mind. I nodded, not sure exactly what the next few weeks or months would bring.

My father pulled a rental car up to the door of the motel and we walked toward it—a detective in front of me and the two ex-cultists on either side both to protect me and to make sure that I didn't float and get the urge to return to the cult. As we piled into the car for a long trip to an airport in Southern California where Moonies couldn't find us, Patrick came up to me and shook my hand, said good-bye.

He turned abruptly and headed back toward the motel. The wheels spun, flinging gravel, as the rented Impala headed out of the parking lot, my father at the wheel.

I sank back in my seat and closed my eyes, resting calmly. A feeling of tremendous gratitude overwhelmed me as I realized that I had been pulled back out of the wrong side of the looking glass. Although I knew that for the next few weeks and months I might press my nose against the mirror, time and again, the Heavenly Kingdom—turned hell—was no longer my domain. The nightmare was over: thanks to the courage of a few, I had been jolted out of my deadly slumber—and awakened to a world that was bright and beautiful again.

epilogue/

From the moment I left the motel and headed home, we were plagued by a number of suspicious events. It started with a series of bogus phone calls and letters which attempted to reach me or intimidate my family. A top Moonie leader who has since been deprogrammed informed me that he had been flown from California to New York to find me.

Within several days of my capture, two large men appeared at the door of my family's home. When a female detective hired to guard my mother opened the door with a chain latch fastened, they broke the chain, knocked down the detective, spat upon her, entered the house, and verbally abused her. They quickly disappeared after she was forced to draw her gun.

After three weeks, I returned to live in my parents' home. People soon started sitting in vans and cars at the bottom of our driveway, shaking their fists at my parents, trailing our cars on occasion. The harassment became so great

229

that my frightened family was guarded by live-in detectives twenty-four hours a day for four months. During this time, people broke into our home twice; although nothing was stolen, the detective verified that our telephone wires had been tampered with. Our burglar alarm system was cut during the first break-in; following the second attempt, somebody damaged the outdoor electrical system. All of these acts of harassment ceased when I began lecturing on American cults.

After my deprogramming in January of 1976, it took a full year of therapy by a specialist in cult-related problems, support from my loving and dedicated family, and continuous effort on my part to adjust to the world—to stop the chanting and singing which continually invaded my mind, to be able to read, reflect, and think again, to relate naturally to men and women, and to feel—to learn how to feel again. Two months after I returned home, I began writing about my experience in a diary, one line at a time, simply for self-understanding. It was out of these fragments, over a thousand pages, that this book evolved.

Since my deprogramming, I have volunteered many hours as a counsellor, helping people through the process of recovery from the same painful ordeal I had experienced. Each case history gave me fire to expose these agonies to the public. Despite cautions from police, I spoke regularly about my experiences on television, in churches, temples, and high schools throughout the Northeast. Some people were shocked, some were curious, and some simply refused to believe that such "fine, clean-cut kids" could use people and allow themselves to be used this way.

During all my talks, I have been repeatedly asked certain questions. The most frequent one has been, Why are cults pulling in millions of young adults today? I can give several basic reasons which account for both the efficiency of conversion techniques and the tremendous susceptability of my generation.

The first factor is the recent development of a technology to influence and control the mind. During the past twenty years, governments throughout the world have been experimenting extensively with these techniques and have employed them with their own agents as well as soldiers and large populations. I recently learned that Green Berets returning from Vietnam underwent deprogrammings in order to return to American society. The Chinese government has employed the "brainwashing" techniques in the "reeducation" camps since the 1950's for the manipulation of millions. These techniques, which are strikingly similar to what I experienced as a cult member, are revealed in a classical study by Yale Psychiatrist Robert Lifton in *Thought Reform and the Psychology of Totalism*.

The second factor lies in my generation's general distrust of society and our rebellion against the over-emphasis on science and technology. We reached adolescence during the height of Vietnam, nuclear weapons, and the ideology of unlimited technological growth. The failure of this ideology resulted in a romantic attempt to "return to nature"; people started engaging in natural or spiritual healing and sought a new ideology to justify their hopes. Unfortunately, they never abandoned the most striking effect of technological values: the search for rapid and sure results. The same people who change "lifestyles" as if they were changing their clothes now consider it possible (and desirable) to learn everything about God, man, and the world in seven days. This reflects both a shallowness of thought and a desperation so typical of my TV-fast-food generation.

The third factor which leads to cult growth is the basic lack of support for young adults from families and institutions. My generation was given the tremendous expectations of happiness and success along with the realities of broken homes, fragmented neighborhoods, and depersonalized schooling. It has often been pointed out that the growth of communes in the sixties was an attempt to form new families—an attempt which failed miserably. It is not accidental that these were followed by the instant communities of cults, many of which, like the Moonies, call themselves the Family.

The Unification Church's witnessing techniques taught me that the most successful tactic in recruiting is to offer friendship and concern. The cult calls this "love bombing." It is remarkably effective. Why is my generation so hungry for love that they can be attracted so easily by saccharine promises? I believe the answer is simply this: we as a people seem to have forgotten how to care about and for each other. We are responsible for the desperation which makes cult promises so attractive. We must relearn how to care and relearn how to listen in a fundamental way. If we don't then I fear that cult terrorism and manipulation will only grow until we actually become the type of One-World Family which the Moonies envision.

The final and most important question I am asked is, Now that we are aware of the problem of mind manipulation, what can we do? We must learn to recognize that the rapid loss of intelligence, the stereotyped gestures and language, the glassy eyes, and the complete lack of individual initiative are indicaters that a sudden, destructive personality change has taken place, probably due to the type of psychological violence described in this book. Not everybody from any one religious cult will exhibit these characteristics, and some people outside of cults will appear this way—such as people in some political groups and many who engage in the new mass-therapies which have become so popular. We must learn to detect and understand these changes. Hopefully, a psychological test will one day emerge to verify these changes objectively and separate the psychological issues from the confusions about cult ideologies or beliefs.

We must inform young adults not to be so naive as to readily and uncritically accept promises of instant bliss and absolute knowledge. We must help them to value themselves and cherish their ability to think responsibly.

In response to those who ask about the future of long-term cult members, I can only warn that their frighteningly robotized behavior may be incurable. John J. Clark, Jr., M.D., Assistant Clinical Professor of Psychiatry at Harvard Medical School, has written about his clinical experience with many of these people who enter this stage of acculturation:

> *This stage may be compared to that of the untreated person with a schizophrenic illness who slides without proper help*

232

> *into a kind of personal degradation which, if unchallenged or untreated, in time finally becomes acculturated and permanent. Anyone trying to nudge a person from this acquired style of thinking and behavior, as we in the mental health field know very well, is going to feel that he is the natural enemy of his own patient. In my opinion, I repeat, by acculturation this new style of thinking may become irreversible.**

There seems to be no escape from cult madness for many members, as evidenced by the fact that in my seven months in the Moonies I only saw one follower able to openly reject the beliefs and leave on his own. A few managed to run away during the night and a few more were dropped off to their parents because cult life made them too physically or emotionally ill to continue. The rest who have left were deprogrammed and successfully returned to the world.

Cult life, as I experienced it, is a one-way passage through a dark and seemingly endless tunnel. If I felt there was hope for those people to either leave the cults or to lead satisfying lives within their groups, if I felt there was something to the promises of light at the end of that tunnel, I could be more optimistic about their fate.

The tragedy of Guyana illustrates one of the many horrifying alternatives for cult members who have pledged their lives to their leader. When the leader loses the vision and all hope for success, the final days of the cult may end in an explosion of violence such as the People's Temple and its powerless followers have suffered.

As time separates me from the hundreds of Moonies I grew to love so much in my cult life, I can only move on, be grateful for my own freedom, and hope that my past experience and my future work will serve to warn about the threat of cult madness.

---

*Statement delivered in August 1976 to the Vermont State Legislature.